Raising Girls

The pleasures, the perils, the pitfalls

Main contributors:

Dr Janet Irwin
Susanna de Vries
Susan Stratigos Wilson

With additional contributions from:

Dr Jean Sparling
Dr John Thearle
Marusia Maccormick
Kate Mascheroni Collins
Erika Pavluk
Jake de Vries

PANDANUS PRESS

ABOUT THE CONTRIBUTORS

DR. JANET IRWIN was born in New Zealand. She studied medicine at the University of Otago, Dunedin, worked in child psychiatry in Edinburgh and in the Student Health Service at the University of Canterbury, Christchurch. Subsequently she became the director of the University of Queensland's Student Health Service and she is now Sexual Harassment Conciliator for the University of Queensland. Dr Irwin raised two girls and a boy and, when her children were in their teens, she became a sole supporting parent. She has been awarded an Order of Australia for 'Services to Women and the Community'.

SUSANNA de VRIES was raised by adoptive parents in London, studied art history in Paris, Madrid and Florence. Formerly married to a psychiatrist, she worked for a period of time in a Family Therapy Clinic. She has written eight books and currently lectures part-time at the University of Queensland (Continuing Education). Susanna has five step-granddaughters. She has been awarded a Churchill Fellowship and an Order of Australia.

SUSAN STRATIGOS WILSON has worked in leading universities and research institutes and was on the staff of the United Nations Division for the Advancement of Women. She is currently a Social Policy Analyst in women's issues. Her blended family consists of seven children and four grandchildren.

DR JEAN SPARLING was born in Britain, graduated in medicine from the University of Sheffield and practised as a GP in London before emigrating to Australia. Dr Sparling has worked as a family practitioner in Victoria, in Tweed Heads and is in general practice in Taringa, Brisbane, with her husband, Dr Clive Sparling. They have three children.

DR JOHN THEARLE was born in Britain, graduated in medicine from the University of Queensland, is currently Senior Lecturer in the University of Queensland's Department of Paediatrics and Child Health at the Mater Children's Hospital, Brisbane.

MARUSIA MACCORMICK studied at Monash, the Australian National and Queensland Universities. She taught English in secondary schools and has wide experience with children from diverse cultural backgrounds. She has two children.

KATE MASCHERONI COLLINS has degrees from the Universities of Essex, London and Queensland, writes for national and international publications and is a Queensland Government Media Adviser. Her household includes resident and semi-resident teenagers.

ERIKA PAVLUK graduated from the University of Queensland and teaches science and mathematics in secondary school. She has been a voluntary worker with the Nursing Mothers Association. Erika has a teenage daughter.

JAKE de VRIES trained as an architect in Holland. He is the designer of this book. Jake raised two girls and two boys. His five granddaughters are featured on the front cover.

CONTENTS

INTRODUCTION

This book, intended for the general reader, contains contributions from three medical practitioners, two school teachers, a policy analyst concerned with women's health and other female issues, a journalist/media adviser and an historian (all parents, grandparents or step-parents). All of us have contributed decades of life-experiences to this book. We aim to share with readers the joys and pleasures of parenting as well as the problems and the perils. We know that nothing else in life brings such pride as sharing a much-loved child's achievements, but nothing brings such pain as a child with severe problems.

In text and pictures we record those precious tender years when little girls are affectionate, cuddly and adorable and describe their passage from total dependence, via the turbulence of adolescence, to adult responsibility.

We have not avoided the 'hard' subjects such as illegal drugs, underage drinking, domestic violence, sexually transmitted infections and the risks from bulimia, anorexia and 'spiritual anorexia' (a total lack of beliefs and aims) that can lead to depressive illness and suicide at a time when teenage girls should have everything to live for.

We emphasise spending time with your teenage daughter and discussing all problems with her rather than merely spending money *on* her. We stress the importance of informed and caring mothering rather than 'competitive' mothering; of calmly and rationally negotiating rules and curfews and pointing out the harmful consequences of poor decisions.

Having written books on women's history, I am well aware how girls used to be undervalued, poorly educated, denied financial independence and married off when young. Luckily, today most young women will live much longer and healthier lives than their counterparts in previous generations. Our world presents girls with greater opportunities but also with new perils, ranging from drug overdose to HIV-AIDS and Hepatitis B.

I am delighted that my step-granddaughters (pictured on the front cover) are so healthy, intelligent and optimistic — sadly two of them have already been introduced to marijuana. Girls now approach maturity in a rapidly changing society where beliefs and family stability are crumbling and where unemployment, recreational drug use, broken marriages and sole supporting mothers have become facts of life. One in three young women will face divorce and custody battles over children and one in five will suffer from depressive illness. It is essential that girls learn to make informed, logical choices from an early age. They should take advantage of the far wider educational and career opportunities available today and, if possible, set their goals to achieve personal and financial independence.

Our book is easy to read and designed for readers from *all* walks of life. It contains real-life stories, illustrations from many different sources and loads of practical ideas which will help *you* to raise healthy, happy, well-balanced and successful girls.

SUSANNA de VRIES, Member of the Order of Australia.

Part 1

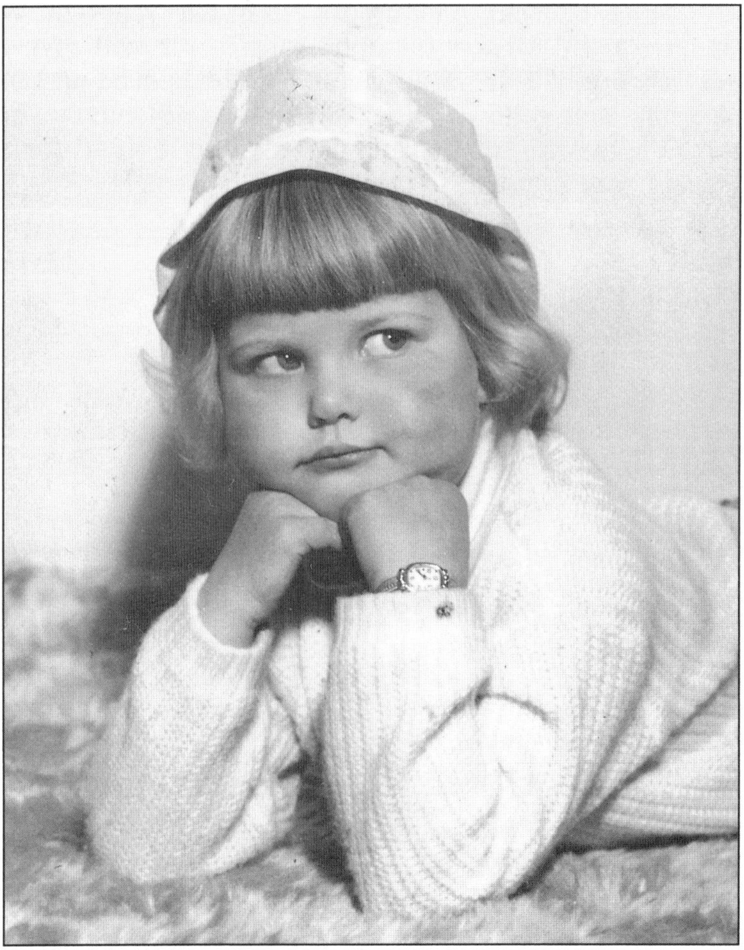

'Thank Heaven for Little Girls'

Title of the song made famous by Maurice Chevalier in *Gigi*

In Part 1 of this book we describe those first ten happy years you will spend with your daughter while guiding her development from babyhood through the toddler stage and her years at primary school. Through enlightening text and enchanting illustrations we show how raising little girls can bring parents tremendous joy and fulfilment.

'Doing it right' during the first ten years of your daughter's life is of vital importance – it will give her every chance of being a happy and well-balanced person in the years that follow. You, as parents, will have a head start in achieving this if your parents 'did it right' for you — if not, you'll just have to work a little harder!

THE TENDER AGE

THE NEWBORN BABY

Being present at the birth of a child is a most unforgettable and special event for those privileged enough to experience it. Like a miracle, the infant starts breathing with perfect timing, opens her eyes and seems to gaze deep within your soul. At that moment you are looking into the eyes of a new human being, uncontaminated by any outside influences and equipped with all the natural potential inherited from her ancestors. A lucky child indeed, if good genes prevail over bad ones. As parents, your challenge will be to complement 'nature' with 'nurture' to the best of your ability. This will need lots and lots of love as well as insight and an understanding of the needs of your newborn baby.

Obviously, lack of experience will make caring for your first-born a greater challenge. To help new parents, there are parenting classes and many excellent books on baby care.[1]

Views on many aspects of child rearing seem to change as the philosophies behind them change over time; however, most guidelines seem to agree on the essential points. When you are confronted with conflicting advice, you may need to rely on your common sense. If you are reasonably well balanced, your instinct will guide you well, as generally you understand your baby best.

Your daughter will spend much of her first few months of life sleeping, feeding and crying, but these are not her only occupations.

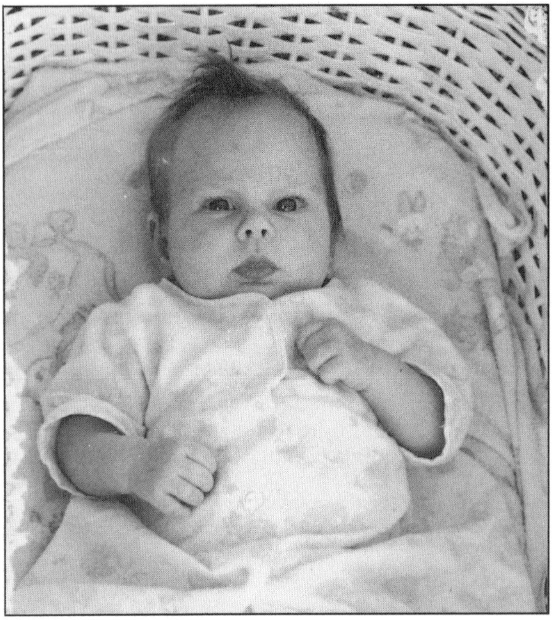

Many things in her environment are already influencing the development of her young mind. During this time, a strong bond will develop between mother and baby — a bond that is further strengthened by frequent physical contact, such as bathing, changing, dressing, cuddling and feeding (preferably breastfeeding). If you make an informed choice *not* to breastfeed, for *whatever* reason, don't feel guilty about this. However, current research suggests the following:

- **Breastfed babies have the potential for a higher intelligence as breast milk contains the Omega-3 fatty acid DHA, important for brain development.[2]**
- **Breast milk contains all the nutrients your baby needs for at least the first six months of her life. It contains antibodies which will help increase your baby's resistance to infection and disease. If she has breast milk only for at least six months it lessens allergy problems.**
- **Breast milk is recommended for lowering the risk of 'Sudden Infant Death Syndrome (SIDS)'.**

Those first few months can be most frustrating for the parents. Few new parents fully realise just *how* often babies cry, especially at night, waking you from sleep you often desperately need. Then there will be feeding problems, nappy rash — possibly accompanied by thrush — which needs medical treatment and vomiting curdled milk, which gives piles of dirty washing. Particularly for previously well-organised career women, the impossibility of planning a daily routine can make new mothers feel totally inadequate. This can be made worse by feelings of postnatal depression and well-meaning but conflicting advice given by parents, in-laws and friends. Accepting this as a temporary but normal phase of parenthood can go a long way to restoring the mother's self-confidence.

Every mother cannot stay home with her baby. Whatever form of child care is chosen (or can be found) it is desirable, though not always possible, that the same caring and dedicated person is there for the child (see also our section on child care on pages 26-27).

Very young babies usually show little separation anxiety. However, no matter how good their child care, some toddlers will protest violently when left by their mothers. Separation anxiety peaks at the age of one year, then wanes gradually over the next couple of years. Every mother is different in her approach and orientations, and so is every baby. If the main care-giver is a nanny or day-care provider, the bond with that person will be broken when arrangements are changed. This could be a traumatic experience for your daughter and might result in increased crying, the only way she can convey her unhappiness. Dad's early involvement with the newborn baby (we will call her Juliet) is of vital importance for developing a successful father-daughter bond. These days, many fathers play an almost equal role in caring for the baby, making the bond between the baby and both parents equally strong.

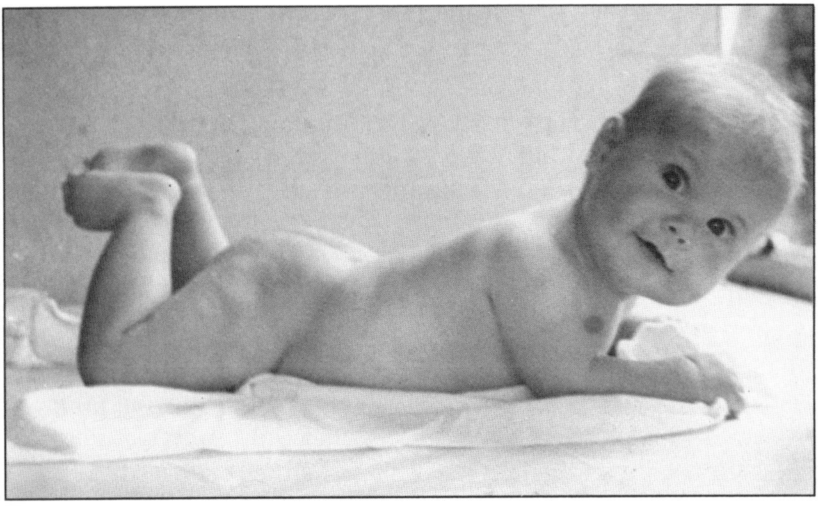

HER MIND AWAKENS

At about six months, your daughter's interest in her surroundings (including her own body) will greatly increase and she will begin to distinguish between the familiar and unfamiliar. Mum and Dad will get smiles, but strangers may often be observed with a degree of apprehension and suspicion. A happy interaction with the mother and the father will soon give little Juliet more confidence and aunts, uncles and older siblings will be accepted.

Towards the end of her first year, Juliet will be able to crawl — her first act of independence. After your daughter's first birthday, her development escalates. Standing up, followed by walking, will soon be within her power. Suddenly she will see the world from a different perspective. Now Juliet's surroundings seem less intimidating and her confidence will increase. Intoxicated by the sheer joy of discovering new and exciting things, she will explore everything within her reach. She has no awareness of the dangers of her surroundings, so your alertness will often be put to the test. Her joy can so easily be spoiled by falling or bumping her head on the table, resulting in screams and floods of tears. It would be much more serious if she poured a cup of hot tea over herself, an accident that *can* happen at this age and could well cause terrible burns.

If not accustomed to being cared for by others by this time, during her second year your daughter can be quite upset at being separated from you. Now she is able to worry about where you are and whether you will return. It can be a difficult time to start handing over your daughter's care to someone else. In certain circumstances, for example, your hospitalisation or work commitments, you will have little choice and your care provider may need extra patience and an understanding of the unsettled behaviour caused by your absence.

During her second year your adorable Juliet will become a handful. Your patience will be tried to the limit. You will often wonder whether your little angel is, in fact, a devil in disguise. Much self-restraint is required not to punish her for what you may perceive to be bad behaviour. Her actions are driven by an instinctive need to explore, discover and examine. By your reactions to her behaviour she will find out what is and isn't allowed. Rather than punishing her, temporarily moving your most valuable, breakable and toxic items out of reach and generally child-proofing your home will protect her (and your breakables) from damage.

To obtain some peace, you may be tempted to use your television as a cheap baby sitter, letting her watch hours of incomprehensible and sometimes disturbing images. At this age she is unlikely to absorb much content. The moving images do have an hypnotic effect, but watching television will rob her of valuable time for active play and exploration. The playpen, not used as frequently these days, is another option for 'getting her out of your way'. Providing she's not confined to the playpen for hours on end and has plenty of toys to play with, this temporary confinement may be a solution. She will probably take great delight in throwing her toys, one by one, out of reach, and then demanding them all back again — an activity that keeps both of you busy, saving you little time.

By now Juliet will have acquired a small vocabulary (boys may be a bit later with their verbal skills). She will discover the power of the word 'NO' and will try to impose her will upon you. Tantrums may follow if she doesn't get her way. Stamping of feet, rolling on the floor or angry, choking shrieks will severely test your 'NO'. It is at this stage that she learns whether you really mean what you say or whether a longer temper tantrum will eventually get her what she wants.

Little girls learn the art of manipulation from an early age. When frustrated in their demands for power and control, most toddlers soon decide a good way of getting attention and their own way is to throw a tantrum. The first time this happens, new parents are amazed by the sheer volume of noise their child's lungs can produce. It also amazes your daughter. Fortunately, at this age she is easily distracted, so the offering of a novel toy or activity can often avoid a major confrontation.

Some toddlers scream, hold their breath, turn purple and seem on the verge of suffocation. Then, after a silence that causes your heart to miss a beat, that dreadful howling and sobbing starts again.

Tantrums begin in the period before your daughter can communicate complex thought via language. Out of fear, misguided love or sheer embarrassment, you may give her exactly what she wants. The result is that she thinks, 'Wow, let's do this again... soon!' Be warned. Unless you act firmly from the start, the 'tantrum racket' will be used by your daughter to blackmail you emotionally into getting her own way… for years and years.

Rehearse an action plan which should *not* include hitting your daughter or yelling. Stay cool even if little Juliet is howling fit to burst her boiler. Your parenting instincts may well invent excuses for her such as, 'It's not her fault, she's got a cold,' or 'My poor darling didn't get her afternoon nap.' Remember it's *your* future sanity we're talking here. Either walk away and ignore your screaming child or pick her up and carry her off to her bedroom, but make sure that you remove any paint or crayons, so she can't make a mess on the walls in revenge.

***Never* let her temper tantrum receive a pay-off. Remove her from her audience (especially in someone else's home). Give her a quick reassuring hug, then leave her alone in a *safe* place. Your daughter's wish to blackmail you emotionally through turning on a temper tantrum will eventually fade.**

Although Juliet is still very young, traces of her femininity start to emerge towards the end of her second year. At this stage fathers and daughters are usually strongly attracted to each other, whilst sons are more likely to be attracted to their mother. Dad is inclined to spoil his daughter more than his son, often being more tolerant and softer with her. This does not stop him from playing fairly rough games, something Juliet delights in with gurgles and shrieks of laughter. With all Mum's softness and warmth, Dad's rough-and-tumble play provides the perfect counterbalance.

By the age of two Juliet may be toilet-trained, but success is *not* guaranteed, since some toddlers realise that it is one area where they have ultimate power. As soon as toilet training becomes a battle of wills, it is best to ease up for a while, as this is one battle that can't be won by confrontation. If *she* doesn't want to perform on her potty you can't make her, whatever *you* do!

If Juliet is not the first-born, older siblings will also start to play a bigger role in her life. Big brother or sister may be jealous of all the attention their little sister gets, but your attitude will determine whether this will develop into full-scale animosity. Once sibling rivalry is firmly established, it can be hard to banish.

HOW *you* CAN HELP

TO AVOID SIBLING RIVALRY

- Make sure that an older sibling has a safe place for treasured possessions. Don't force the older sibling to share toys with Juliet.
- Take time to do special activities with the older child.
- Show appreciation when an older sibling helps you.
- Limit the older sibling's time and responsibility in caring for Juliet.
- Visitors should be asked to make a fuss of the older sibling before they enthuse over the new baby.
- Treat each child as an individual — *never* make comparisons.
- Avoid taking 'sides' in fights or arguments — allow them to solve their own differences. Ignore disharmony as far as possible. Act as a mediator only if real harm is looming.
- Catch them being good, that is, notice and give praise when both siblings are relating well.

THE POWER OF LANGUAGE

During her third year, Juliet's language skills will develop rapidly and form the basis for logical thought, abstract reasoning and eventually intelligent conversation, making her a social creature. Interaction with other adults and children increases. She will try to imitate others and be an unbearable chatterbox at times, asking more questions than you can answer, making more demands than you are able to meet. To you, much of her conversation and many of her questions may seem trivial, but to her they may be matters of great importance. If possible, give her your full attention and respond positively. At other times you will be busy and need to tell her this. She will accept this if she knows that later on she will have your full attention. However, if you are 'too busy' too often, a barrier to future communication will develop, and Juliet may stop coming to you. As she is developing the ability to reason, you can often explain your decisions when she asks for things. This is a good age to start making compromises and agreements; for example, 'If you help by putting all your blocks back in the box, I can finish my job. Then I'll have time to read you a story'. This doesn't mean that you have to give in to all her demands or that you have to explain yourself *all* the time but do set aside some special time for her.

Dedicated parents are tempted to do anything in their power to maximise their child's learning from a very early age. They buy many educational toys to stimulate their child's cognitive development and books on increasing their child's intelligence so she has an edge when she starts school. They may spend many hours daily providing an environment where their child is bombarded with visual, auditory and tactile stimulation.

Does this have any value when Juliet is already so busy absorbing many impressions in her everyday life? Certainly, you may give her an intellectual advantage which will put her ahead of her classmates at preschool, but there is little evidence that such excessive stimulation pays off in the long run. Unfortunately, sometimes it causes anxiety for both of you, which could harm your relationship and result in a negative attitude towards learning.

This does not mean that you should make no attempt at stimulating your daughter's curiosity for learning. While you are both enjoying it, it can be a positive and worthwhile experience. Expensive and specialised equipment is rarely needed. There is no money to be made from advertising this fact, but everyday household equipment and activities are often the best learning material. Pictures, cut-outs and letters provide visual stimuli; the radio will produce sound and some inexpensive push and pull toys will give muscle control. You may also be able to make your own educational toys. When she gets a bit older, a few more sophisticated educational toys could be bought, but don't overdo it! Setting the correct number of places at the table, measuring and counting while cooking or shopping, or filling various containers with sand or water are extremely valuable activities to give understanding of basic mathematical ideas. Reading to Juliet and talking about the book's pictures or discussing a day's events before bedtime provide a great foundation for language learning.

DISCOVERING GENDER DIFFERENCES

Juliet will become more preoccupied with her own body and, given a chance, will discover and wonder about the differences between her body and that of any available male.

If she has been brought up to feel comfortable with all parts of her body, she is bound to ask questions about the differences and the reason for them. Matter-of-fact answers and open discussion set the stage now for easier communication about sexual development and reproduction later, when this topic often becomes more emotionally charged. She may not fully understand all that you tell her, but will absorb what she wants to know. More importantly, she will learn that this topic may be discussed if she needs to know more.

Gender differences will show in other ways. The difference between girls and boys before the age of two is not very obvious. After this, interests, aptitudes and behaviour separate both sexes further. Juliet tends to be more verbal and inquisitive but less aggressive than Romeo. She may start to flirt, particularly in the presence of her father or other male persons to whom she is drawn. Often her preference for toys will differ too. This may partly come about due to social expectation — parents may provide her only with toys that they feel are suitable for a girl. It has been found that even when given the same types of toys as boys, such as blocks and trains, girls tend to play with them differently. You should give Juliet the chance to play with Lego as well as dolls. A lack of opportunity to play with construction toys is one reason that girls, on average, do less well in maths and science subjects. You never know, she might be destined to become an architect or engineer.

From babyhood onwards Juliet will receive pleasure from touching her genital area. This innocent self-pleasuring is quite harmless and should cause no concern. However, as soon as she is old enough to understand, she must be told to refrain from such behaviour when other people are present. If your little daughter touches her genitals frequently, it may be an indication that she is bored, feels insecure and hence unloved. Often all she needs is your attention — many kisses and hugs are vital during this important stage of her emotional and physical development.

If your daughter touches her genital area excessively, an irritation could be another reason. If you suspect that this could be due to an infection, check immediately with your doctor, because it could have serious consequences if not properly attended to.

IMPORTANT POINTS

SAFETY TIPS FROM A PAEDIATRICIAN

Dr John Thearle, Senior Lecturer in the University of Queensland's Department of Paediatrics and Child Health and some concerned parents give the following practical hints on baby and child care.

- Lie your baby down to sleep on her *back* rather than her tummy. Do *not* overheat her room (which must be smoke-free) and keep a window open, so that fresh air circulates around her. If you can, breastfeed your baby. These points are all recommended in the latest research into Sudden Infant Death Syndrome.[3]
- There is no firm evidence that proprietary medicines help babies with colic. Repositioning your baby to make her more comfortable, nursing her, gently massaging her tummy and her back help soothe colic pains, which occur mainly in the evening ('sunset colic') and in the first three months of her life.
- Before talking to your family doctor or paediatrician, write down *all* your sick child's symptoms, body temperature and any questions you want to ask. Take a pencil and paper with you to note down *all* the instructions the doctor provides.
- You can buy from the chemist special syringes which measure the correct dose of any liquid medicine. Use one of these to squirt the medicine into the mouth of your daughter. Forcing medicine into her mouth with a spoon often means that some dribbles down her face. Foul-tasting medicine tastes far *less* bad if a toddler or child (but not a baby) has first sucked an ice cube.
- More household accidents happen to toddlers when their parents are busy talking on the phone than at any other time. **Don't let toddlers out of your sight** once you pick up the phone.
- Your daughter's toys should have embroidered eyes, not glass or button eyes, which can easily be picked off and swallowed.
- Keep all poisonous items out of your daughter's reach. Swap toxic cleaning things from the cupboard under the sink (where a toddler can easily find and swallow them) with tinned foods and unbreakables from the top shelves of your kitchen cupboards or buy and fit inexpensive child-proof locks for cupboard doors. Power point guards are also available from some stores.

MILESTONES IN YOUR DAUGHTER'S DEVELOPMENT

THESE ARE ONLY INTENDED AS GUIDELINES. REMEMBER, EACH CHILD'S DEVELOPMENT DIFFERS GREATLY

AT THREE MONTHS

- Lying on her tummy, she can push herself up on her arms. She will have reasonable head control and will smile at you, making your heart miss a beat with love for her.
- She will be able to hold on to a small object for a limited time.

AT SIX MONTHS

- She can sit up totally unaided for a short time and can hold a toy or move it from one hand to another.
- While lying on her tummy, she can push herself up and roll onto her back. She plays with and even sucks her fingers and toes.

AT NINE MONTHS

- She can support herself on hands and knees and possibly crawl.
- She can sit unaided for a fairly long time and is fascinated by the world around her. Move all breakables and create a child-free zone, as she can now pick up small objects, break them and put them in her mouth. Be aware of the dangers. On the positive side, she can now eat a biscuit unaided and hold a cup or bottle.

- She may pull herself up and stand while holding on to the wall or furniture.

AT ONE YEAR

- She may be able to toddle or walk unaided.
- She will respond when you call her by name and may even say a few recognisable words.
- She can hold on to, give or receive small objects; watch that she doesn't swallow them.

AT EIGHTEEN MONTHS

- She can turn the pages of a book, hold a pencil or crayon in her hand and scribble on sheets of paper or on your walls!
- She can hold a spoon and feed herself without making *too* much of a mess.
- Be warned, the 'Terrible Twos' start from now on.

AT TWO YEARS

- She can throw and catch a ball, thread large beads and put together a simple jigsaw puzzle. The 'Terrible Twos' and temper tantrums continue.
- She can formulate simple sentences like, 'I don't want to' and 'Why not?' She needs limits set, against which she will rebel as a natural part of growing up. She may be toilet-trained. Don't worry if she's not.

AT THREE YEARS

- She can stack eight or more building blocks that don't topple and fasten buttons and large zips.
- She may be able to draw letters and recognisable characters and will ask endless questions about herself and the world beyond. Now is the time for her to separate fantasy from reality.

BECOMING A PERSON

THE FIRST STEPS TO INDEPENDENCE

Remember, we are seeing Juliet growing up in the ideal environment. During the first three years of her life she had two parents, one her full-time care-giver, the other (most likely her father) sufficiently involved with her upbringing to be adored by the child. Probably there were other children. In other words, we are talking about the 'perfect' nuclear family — don't be cynical, such families do still exist.

During these first three years, you have taken care of your daughter's emotional and physical development to the best of your ability, caring for her yourself as much as circumstances permitted. You have encouraged her to explore. You dealt with her kindly and

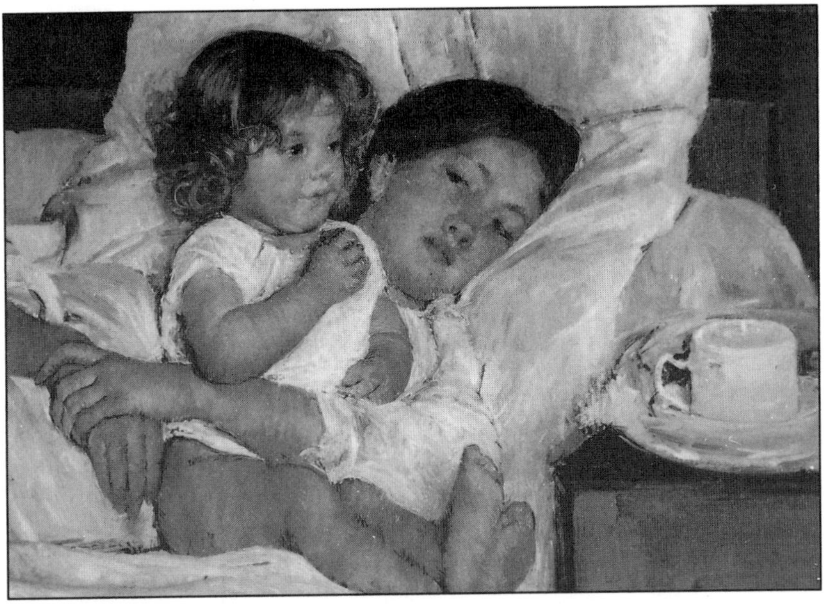

Mary Cassatt, an American artist who worked in Paris and died in France in 1926, is famous for the feeling of tenderness between mothers and daughters in her portraits.

with understanding but were firm when she misbehaved. You guided her towards greater independence and now are worthy of her love, affection and respect.

Does it follow that, as a three-year-old, she is a perfect child, certain to grow up a well-balanced person?

No, of course it doesn't! However, your daughter has reached the stage in her life at which she should be allowed to become more independent. You have to be prepared to move away a little and let her practise being herself.

HER INSATIABLE CURIOSITY

Juliet has learned the rudiments of language and is now capable of deeper thought. She will ask more in-depth questions about various things — how they are made, how they work, where they come from.

Due to increased self-awareness, she may ask more pertinent questions about herself and will observe with increasing interest the difference between her own body and that of other people, both female and male. Continue responding to her questions as honestly and openly as you can — each time you explain she will understand a little more. Do keep in mind that her comprehension is still limited and long lectures on the facts of life (or any other subject, for that matter) will only confuse or bore her. The best way to check what she already understands is by asking her what she thinks or remembers from what you have previously told her.

Your attitude to her questions continues to be of great importance. She will sense any uneasiness or embarrassment and will know if you answer in an evasive or dismissive way. Don't miss this most important opportunity to keep building trust and openness between yourself and your daughter. Once a wall of silence has been created, it becomes very hard to break it down.

Juliet's sexual curiosity may not be fully satisfied with answers only. One day you might find her and Jamie from next door in the back garden, examining each other's bodies. It's a normal process of satisfying curiosity with tangible evidence and is quite innocent. If it upsets you, distract the children by providing some other activity, without making them feel guilty. Reprimands or punishment will ensure she'll try not to get caught next time, at best, or,

worse, may result in long-term feelings of guilt and shame about her body.

By now the bond between Juliet and her father has been further strengthened — she might feel even closer to him than to her mother. If she is the girl we think she is (and if you are the Dad we think you are), she adores you and can't wait for you to come home from work. She plays games with you, loves it when you throw her high up in the air and finds your stories more exciting than those Mum tells (or is it just your tone of voice?). On weekends you may take her out for walks or to the playground. You are her hero, her very best friend and she is bound to be in love with you. Make the most of this time because it so short. It's amazing how quickly she'll grow up and find someone else to love.

An ironic view of the father-daughter relationship. Freely translated from a Dutch cabaret song.

On those lovely Saturdays,
Out there in the sun,
Walking with my daughter,
Was such tremendous fun.
    Feeding ducks and coots,
    Picking flowers in the woods.
    Look, your dress, it's green with moss!
    How dirty are your hands!
    Mummy will be very cross.

Daddy was her hero,
Daddy was her friend.
He was God and Santa Claus
In nearly perfect blend.
    Is doggie giving you a fright?
    It's okay, that doggie doesn't bite.
    The dog didn't even snarl,
    On that lovely Saturday,
    As I was walking with my darl.

Pretty girl is growing up,
Little rose in bud.
Dad must chase away that boy:
Hands off, you useless dud!
    Do you have that problem too?
    What do you think, of course I do!
    No use praying there in church,
    On that lovely Saturday,
    She will leave you in the lurch.

She may well be pregnant soon,
Probably today.
That painter could be the loon,
Or that bloke from Byron Bay.
    Dad preaches and gets wild:
    That dog will bite you, child!
    Dad turns purple in the face
    When she ignores his pleas.
    It's yet another hopeless case.

Father is a hypocrite,
Father is a dill,
Only good for earning money,
The rest amounts to nil.
    Perhaps once again I may,
    On some lovely Saturday,
    Walk out there in the sun,
    With my daughter — hand in hand.
    Wouldn't that be tremendous fun?

CHILD CARE: A REALITY OF MODERN LIFE

At three, or maybe even much earlier, Juliet will go to 'kindy' or any other form of child care that you consider right for her. Although you may have looked forward to this time, you will have mixed feelings if she has been at home with you most of the time. You will no longer be the hub around which your daughter's life revolves. Now the outside world will take a greater role in her further development, both emotionally and intellectually. Interaction with other people will be added to your continuing care. The importance of your care has not diminished, but the quality of time together will become more important than the quantity.

It can be a big step for your daughter to go into child care. Preparation should take place if prolonged separations have been minimal so far. You know how Juliet responded when a relative or a friend looked after her while you went shopping or be at the hairdresser. This should give you an idea of how much preparation she'll need for coping with longer separations. Often it's Mum who finds the separation hardest, suffering mixed feelings of guilt and relief as she leaves her daughter in child care. Reassure yourself that Juliet will derive great benefit from attending any form of well-accredited child care.

Investigate the quality and accreditation of care that will be provided and make sure you are satisfied that it meets your requirements. Guidelines to quality care are freely available, and we strongly suggest that you refer to these before making a decision.[1]

Child care should complement Juliet's development at home and should be in line with your philosophy. Accredited centres are run by qualified personnel (as required by law). It is worth carefully investigating private care arrangements, particularly for the very young. Even qualified carers vary in their expertise and temperaments and in some cases may not meet your expectations. For your daughter's well-being and your own peace of mind, be prepared to contact the centre of your choice to discuss and resolve problems as soon as they arise. You may need to be prepared to seek out more appropriate care, if problems cannot be resolved.

At 'kindy' and other child care centres play is the predominant activity — play is a vital part of your daughter's development. Playing with old or toy kitchen tools, letter blocks, or dressing-up clothes all help her to make sense of the world and her place in it.

For a wide variety of reasons, connected with finance or maintaining your career structure, you may have gone back to work long before Juliet is three. In order to maintain a close bond with your daughter, you will have made a special effort to relate well to her during the time you *can* be with her. During that time you will have given her the maximum attention possible.

Juliet's unique genetic make-up may very well make her more independent, extroverted and socially at ease by the age of two than Jamie from next door is at the age of four. To avoid the shyness which often plagues young children (especially only children), never consider it 'cute' if she hides behind you and refuses to speak to visitors. Do not provide excuses for this. Extreme shyness will give her problems at school and may lead to being bullied. Teach her from an early age to put out her hand to visitors and say 'Hullo, my name is Juliet.' Praise and reward her when she does this, so that it becomes second nature: you will make life easier for her in future.

TOYS, GAMES AND FAIRY TALES

To spoil your daughter, you might be tempted to buy her one of the very sophisticated toys now available; for instance, a doll that can walk, talk and perhaps even eat and excrete, presented in the most immaculate clothes and jewellery. Although Juliet will be thrilled with her present at first, it is likely she will soon leave it lying in a corner and return to her much cheaper, more creative toys — the battered doll she can dress, those things she can take apart and put together again or the cardboard boxes and old curtains she can use to build cubby houses. Simple, everyday items will be her favourites; play dough, finger paint, clay, sand and water. Her sophisticated new doll is too complete and perfect, leaving little scope for creativity and imagination. So, save your money. There are probably many items lying around the house that will give your daughter more pleasure and generate much more creativity than the most expensive toys can provide. If you have money to spend, build a sandpit or buy some Lego. These will provide hours of pleasure.

We strongly recommend that when you buy toys, you take no chances with your daughter, always considering safety and suitability. Safety information is readily available and manufacturers are required to supply warnings if toys are unsuitable for children below a certain age. Also be aware of toys that have been found unsafe and are withdrawn from the market.

Experts are divided as to whether destructive toys, such as daggers or guns, have a harmful effect and to what extent they can induce violence. Girls often show little interest in these, so this may not be an issue, but our own opinion is that these toys don't contribute anything positive to the child's learning experience.

Games provide an ideal medium for teaching social interaction and simple games can be played with your children from a very young age. It is almost impossible that these days your daughter will not be exposed to computer games. Although there are some high quality programs of educational value, many games contain elements of violence. At this age, interaction with others and the development of motor skills are very important and cannot be developed by interaction with a computer. So computer time should be limited.

What about fairy tales? Bruno Bettelheim has suggested that fairy tales are the best food for the childish imagination, because in their traditional folk form they capture the young hero's struggle to overcome adversities and emerge as a triumphant self.[2]

Most traditional fairy tales contain some cruelty or violence: the wolf eats Grandma, the Ugly Sisters are cruel to Cinderella — plus all those terrifying giants. Somehow, those timeless fairy tales by Hans Christian Anderson are still greatly admired and the cruelty to the Little Mermaid and the Ugly Duckling is taken for granted by little listeners. It seems children can accept a fair amount of bad things happening, as long as the perpetrator is punished in the end.

Of course, there are plenty of non-violent children's stories, too. The old favourites, such as books by Beatrix Potter, Dr Seuss and the stories of Winnie the Pooh by A. A. Milne, are still very popular. There are also many excellent books for children in bookshops and libraries, written by contemporary authors, which entertain as well as educate.

Before Juliet has learned to read, she will be thrilled when you tell her stories or read them to her. Storytelling provides a unique interaction between child and parent and has the edge on many other forms of entertainment. The author of this chapter remembers the thrill she experienced as a child when her mother sat down beside her, opened a children's book and continued the story interrupted the previous night, just before the most exciting moment — the anticipation of what would happen next in the story had been almost unbearable.

By the age of six, your daughter may be starting to read for herself, opening up the exciting world of books even further. Listening to your storytelling will certainly stimulate her wish to be able to read her own favourite stories. Initially, you may read with her, preferably out of illustrated books with simple text, helping her to interpret the more difficult words.

Introducing your daughter to the world of books and encouraging her to read when she is ready for it, are the most valuable contributions you can make to her early education and happiness, and fulfilment in later life. In spite of the vast increase in electronic means of conveying information (television, the Internet, CD-ROMs), the book is bound to remain the most accessible and user-friendly source of knowledge and enjoyment for a long time yet.

TELEVISION — FRIEND OR FOE?

Apart from a few excellent educational programs for kids, such as '*Sesame Street*' and '*Playschool*,' most TV programs have few redeeming features. It is the nature of television-watching, not so much the content, that is the *real* enemy of childhood development. The deeply-ingrained habit of spending hours and hours sitting down watching TV or videos, can lead to shy, withdrawn or grossly overweight children and may cause reduced attention span at school. Some doctors believe that too much TV watching is one contributory factor to attention-deficit disorder (ADD). Television robs children of the opportunity to play actively, to develop their imagination and interact with other people. Even nature programs and documentories, good in themselves as information and entertainment for children, remain poor substitutes for listening to story-telling, playing games or other forms of direct interaction.

Another concern is that children are seen by commercial concerns as captive targets for television advertising, thereby creating unreasonable desires for toys, other material goods and junk foods.

For children of ten and beyond, the value of watching most TV programs is marginal and should be limited to those selected and approved by you in advance. It can be invaluable to watch certain programs with your daughter, giving you both the opportunity to discuss what is seen. A child will interpret TV violence and casual sex as reflecting real life. It has been suggested that most of today's children will have seen some 12,000 murders on TV and video games by the time they leave school. You may need to explain violent acts on TV in the context of the story. Your daughter cannot be completely sheltered from watching acts of violence, explicit sex, rape or other undesirable images, but if she doesn't understand their relevance, your presence can be important, as you can discuss and explain to her what is happening.

The consequence of young children being exposed to sex, violence and crime on television is their loss of innocence early in life. Can they mentally cope with all the horrors they are watching? There is plenty of evidence that 'copycat' crime is committed by adolescents as a result of watching similar acts of crime and violence on television and video and computer games. This violence is often committed by the good-looking hero as well as by the

villain, encouraging children to see it as an acceptable way of resolving problems, rather than by more peaceful methods.

Even if we can convince *you* of the uselessness or even the destructive effect of watching far too much television, it doesn't mean that you can suddenly drag your four- or five-year-old daughter away from the screen without causing major upheaval. The habit can be difficult to break. Let's be honest, you may be slightly addicted yourself. A total ban (probably only possible if you sell the set) may result in her finding a friend's house where viewing is unrestricted. Try moderation and carefully select the best programs for your daughter to watch. Avoid using television-watching as a reward for good work or behaviour, as this tends to enhance its desirability and importance.

DISCIPLINE — IS IT STILL RELEVANT TODAY?

Some associate the word 'discipline' with negative images of harsh treatment and absolute obedience. We, however, see discipline as teaching your daughter good social skills, a sense of right and wrong and self-discipline. Certainly very relevant today! Bringing up children without discipline is like sailing a ship without a rudder.

The liberal views on discipline after the second world war were greatly influenced by Dr Benjamin Spock's book, *Baby and Child Care.* Often blamed for the licentious hippie lifestyle, even he eventually admitted he had gone too far.

These days it is known that children are happier with definite limits and a clear understanding of acceptable behaviour. Most of the time, Juliet will want to do the right thing and will do so if you clearly teach her what you expect. Give her a reason for rules if possible; it makes her realise rules are not pointless or arbitrary. 'In our house we don't jump on the chairs because they get broken.' She needs to know what to expect if she breaks the rule. The consequence of breaking the rule needs to be logical. If she keeps jumping on the chair, a slap is not a logical consequence. Tell her she has a choice: 'Juliet, you need to sit quietly on the chair or go outside to jump.' At times, she needs to test if you really mean what you say. She may continue jumping and you may need to physically carry her outside.

Make consequences of misbehaviour immediate and inevitable. Once she knows that by ignoring you, throwing a big enough tantrum, or whining long enough, you will eventually give in, she will persist until you do. A rule not important enough to enforce is not a rule. Be consistent — it's not fair to reprimand her today because she's running around the house screaming when normally that is allowed. Tell her the reason if today's rules are different. 'I've got a terrible headache. Please make your noise outside today', or 'We are expecting visitors, I don't want your toys on the lounge-room floor this morning. Please keep them in the playroom.'

Modelling the behaviour you want is by far the most effective way to teach manners, standards and self-discipline. Practise what you preach! Do you back up your statement that study is important by continuing your own education? Do *you* turn off the TV when your program is over? Do *you* manage your money wisely, spending judiciously and saving regularly? Maybe you rant and rave about the terrors of drugs while you smoke, drink and pop pills for every minor ailment? Do you try every fad diet while insisting Juliet eats her meat and vegetables?

IS JULIET SOMETIMES DISHONEST?

Dishonesty is of major concern to parents. Young children lie without meaning to, making up fantasies or exaggerating the truth to give adults a version of what they *wished* had happened rather than what did happen. Explain the difference between truth and fantasy. Older children often 'bend the truth' if they fear punishment, and these are the lies that upset parents most. Examine *why* they lied and, if you punish them, make sure it is something connected with their misdemeanour. Don't implant in their minds that they will turn into criminals. You can even ask them (or their siblings) what punishment they think they should receive — you may be surprised how tough kids can be on other kids!

As regards dishonesty, example speaks louder than words. Be a good example to your daughter! When you find something of value, do you make a *real* effort to trace the owner? Do you leave your name and address if you accidentally dent a parked car? Or do you 'borrow' things from work and boast about evading tax?

It can be a shock the first time your little innocent steals. You need to establish that she understands what she has done. You may need to *clearly* explain she has done wrong, and why. If she fully understands her misdeed, she needs to face the consequences. Don't yell or slap her. There is absolutely no place in modern discipline for inflicting physical pain, denying food or ordering long periods of isolation in her room. Taking your daughter back to the shop to apologise and waiting while she *personally* returns the stolen item or making her 'earn' the money she took out of your purse by doing jobs around the house would be suitable penalties. Make these punishments fair and just and a logical consequence of *her* actions; without doubt, it is the correct way of disciplining her.

If your daughter is stealing, she may be exploring whether there are really negative consequences to her behaviour. Perhaps she wants to find out whether you would let her 'get away with it'. Maybe she needs attention from you — she may see you as someone often too busy to talk to (many kids feel that negative attention is better than no attention at all). Maybe she wants the independence of having some money but has no way to earn it. It will be useful to have a talk with her to find out the real reason for her behaviour. Once you know the cause you can do something about it.

THE WORLD BEYOND

INDEPENDENCE, CREATIVITY AND SELF-ESTEEM

Around the age of five or six, your daughter has reached the middle years of childhood, the stage usually referred to as the school years or the latency period. Her independence and gender identity will start to develop at this time of her life. She will also become more and more receptive to all kinds of learning.

Although she may not always admit it, for a number of years she will be greatly influenced by your way of life, your values and your behaviour. Rebellion comes later in her teens, but now, during the years of relative psychological calmness, she will adopt and accept her parents' standards, either consciously or subconsciously. Juliet will almost certainly adopt (and accept as normal) many of your attitudes to life; both the obvious ones, such as your religious, political and ethical beliefs, and the more subtle, such as your taste in music and clothes, phobias, attitude towards money and education. Less desirable habits and attitudes are also easily adopted. If you are a television addict, it will be hard to keep her away from the set. If you quarrel rather than settle differences more maturely, she will become quarrelsome too.

With her desire for

learning comes the sheer pleasure of creativity and accomplishment. Showing off the drawing she's just finished, completing a puzzle or building a complex Lego structure gives her enormous joy. Your response to these accomplishments is of utmost importance. Admire her achievements. Even if the standard of her work is below your expectations, words of praise and encouragement are most important — there is always something positive to say. Negative comments will discourage her, inhibit her creativity and undermine her self-esteem. Of course, cautious suggestions as to how she could further improve her work are in place. A positive attitude towards your daughter's learning in general is much more fruitful than negativism. It will also raise her self-esteem. If her achievements are frequently disapproved of, she will lose interest in learning and creativity and eventually resort to idleness and mischief.

At this stage of her life, it is most important that your daughter's self-esteem is developing along with her independence. If she has a low opinion of herself, you and her teacher(s) must help her to increase her self-esteem before it is too late — it will help her cope with the pressures of life now and, even more so, during adolescence. Self-esteem helps her fight off 'stranger danger'. It gives her the confidence to say **NO** if a stranger offers her a present or a lift in a car. If she has low self-esteem when entering her teens, she can be seriously handicapped in asserting herself and persisting in saying no if she is unhappy about someone's unacceptable demands.

It is vital in today's world that Juliet learns the difference between 'good' and 'bad' touching. Here again, self-esteem will be paramount. If she feels uncomfortable with the way an adult or a much older child is touching or fondling her, she must have the confidence to say, 'Please stop. I don't like that'. If the touching continues and she becomes annoyed or worried, she must have the confidence to seek help or tell someone.

THE TIME FOR FORMAL LEARNING

Above all, the years between six and ten (and beyond) are the years for learning. Your daughter spends at least thirty hours per week on formal learning at school and many more hours in absorbing knowledge by reading books, playing games, communicating with parents

Schoolgirl 130 years ago

Lucy's first school day (1994)

and friends and, we reluctantly agree, even by watching certain programs on television. Her capacity for learning is now at its peak — she is able to absorb an astounding amount of knowledge with relative ease.

You may notice a change in the way Juliet solves problems. Previously she may have needed actual objects to help her solve problems (for example, counting on her fingers) but now she is increasingly able to visualise them. On average, she may have more difficulty with mathematics than the boys in her class, but her verbal skills tend to develop faster than those of her male classmates. It appears that this is to some degree due to parental expectations and opportunities she's had at home.

Formal learning at school may be the most important part of her cognitive input, but do not underestimate the value of *your* input at home. Why do children from intellectual parents seem so much brighter than those of less educated ones? Often there is little or no difference in intelligence, but everyday conversation and other verbal interaction make the difference, as does the value *you* attach to learning. Although often not directly involved in conversations, subconsciously a child will assimilate ideas and facts that were discussed. If the conversations at home mainly concern mundane events, rather than exchanges of ideas and knowledge, this is all that Juliet absorbs — and she will be the poorer for it.

Schools these days have to cater for students with an increasingly wide range of ability, from those bound for university to those with severe learning disabilities. The majority of students now complete high school, whereas in the past only a minority did. This has often resulted in the impression that increasing numbers of students have inadequate literacy and numeracy skills, while in fact the actual numbers are not changing greatly. At different times, philosophies do change, from a time where facts were all-important to a time where processes (the 'how to do it') were emphasised. In the present climate, both are seen as important.

The type of discipline in schools has also changed. There was a time when students had automatic respect for authority. During the sixties, people started to question authority, which had considerable implications for the behaviour of students in schools. These days, behaviour management is based on teaching students that they have certain rights and certain responsibilities and that not fulfilling their responsibilities leads to undesirable consequences. It is a harder process for teachers. Sometimes behaviour may seem more unruly; however, it is an important learning process during which students (ideally) actually become responsible for their own behaviour rather than behaving correctly only while an authority figure is present.

Teachers often experience that children from broken homes have greater difficulty conforming to class rules and attaining desired learning outcomes. Their behaviour and performance often improve when their teacher manages to win their respect and admiration — a difficult, but not impossible, task. Sadly, if your daughter is surrounded by unruly classmates, it will affect her performance, too. A highly motivated peer group can be a real advantage. Endeavour to choose a school where there are pupils with dedicated and motivated parents, who are concerned about their children's education. It is well worth spending time checking out the policies and atmosphere of *all* the schools in your area before deciding which one is best for Juliet. A school that is not too large, with a caring and stimulating atmosphere, tends to enhance student performance.

Ethel Spowers made this coloured linocut of children playing in the 1930s.

LEISURE TIME: FRIENDS, SPORTS AND GAMES

Despite the strong emphasis on formal education during her latency years, the importance of leisure time should not be underrated. It is an important time for interaction with her friends: playing games, being involved in sport, in the performing arts and in a range of other creative activities.

Parents want the best for their daughter and, to ensure she has a wide range of experiences and opportunities, are often tempted to over-schedule out-of-school activities in evenings and on weekends. The high expectations and continuous rushing about can be very stressful. It is important that Juliet has enough spare time to plan her own activities, listen to music, talk to her friends or read books.

During this time, Juliet is finding her independence, gradually growing away from you. Her friends become more and more important. She may have many friends, but often only one or two close enough to share all her secrets. Her problem may be that

today's friends are not tomorrow's. Who is 'in' their clique or secret club may change daily and the reason for 'falling out' is often not clear — even the one now isolated may not know.

She will play games or sport with her friends. They will show each other pictures of their role models: heroes or heroines from sport, film or television. She may boast about her parents (at least in your absence) and show off her new clothes and shoes, but she does not (yet) have the confidence to wear outrageous gear to give her a personal identity. Juliet prefers to be, and to look, like everybody else in her group. Your choice of clothes may not be acceptable to her, and much drama may be avoided if you go shopping together, allowing her to choose with the understanding that you have the final say, or allowing her to choose from a range acceptable to you.

Although it is a period for intense interaction with others, Juliet also needs time for privacy, to withdraw in the world of her own fantasies or to absorb the fantasies of others. Reading, drawing or painting pictures, working out puzzles and writing her own stories are all activities she can pursue by herself. The need for solitude differs from child to child. If Juliet is an introvert, she needs to have more time to herself than her extroverted contemporary.

Inevitably, your daughter will spend leisure time using the computer. Whether we like it or not, the computer has increasingly become a part of life and many children are introduced to it at an early age. Some parents may be quite awed at the ease with which their youngster takes to computers. Unlike watching television, at least a computer needs her active involvement, whether she plays games, does word processing, extracts information from CD-ROMs or has already mastered surfing the Internet. The Internet is a mixed blessing. Access to information has no limit but can include some deplorable subjects: child pornography, making explosives and making designer drugs are just a few examples. On the positive side, it provides a wealth of data for study and research. Once again, your involvement and supervision are most important. At this age computer games will probably be of most interest to her. As with TV programs, computer games range from the very good to horrific, violent trash with no redeeming features.

GENDER DIFFERENTIATION

Between the ages of six and nine Juliet firmly establishes her gender. Although there is some overlap, her interests gradually become distinct from those of boys. Girls typically enjoy dressing up, often in combination with role-playing. Before the age of six they acted out fairy tales, now they prefer to represent their favourite pop stars and television characters, accompanied by appropriate music. Fancy dress parties are also highly popular.

She may have become interested in make-up, applying lipstick and painting her fingernails and toenails in the most bizarre colours. You may feel she is far too young for make-up, but your strong disapproval now may cause her to go into extremes in her teens. During this time boys of her own age are not within Juliet's social circle and mostly looked upon as inferior and 'awkward' beings. She may, however, have a crush on an older boy or a male school teacher or be secretly in love with her idol, such as a pop star or sporting hero.

Girls may also differ from boys in the sports they prefer. They may be just as competitive as boys, but generally prefer swimming, netball, tennis and athletics to the more aggressive contact sports. There are plenty of girls, however, who feel quite put out when not given the opportunity to play these 'boys' sports'. Team work becomes increasingly important, not just in sport but also in games, at birthday parties and with activities in their 'secret' clubs.

Horse riding may be one of Juliet's favourite activities — it is the love for the animal and the wish to be out in the open that makes riding so appealing to girls. It is a healthy activity and will develop her motor skills and coordination. Gymnastics are also excellent for developing coordination. Many girls love ballet classes, but they must be watched to make sure they don't start dieting to achieve a ballerina figure — which could lead to serious eating disorders.

THE NEED TO GIVE JULIET RESPONSIBILITY

Helping around the house, taking care of her own room, feeding and walking the dog are all tasks Juliet can perform from about seven years onwards. Feeling that she is useful and making important contributions to the household allows her to feel grown-up and competent. You may well be able to do many jobs quicker yourself, but letting her know this will undermine her self-esteem. Remember that having the job completed is a minor goal; making her feel useful, responsible and capable is the major goal. She may complain that you expect too much, but sparing her from all tasks and responsibilities means she will miss out on learning many important skills. Expecting others to always do everything for her is not a good way to start later relationships.

Despite occasional grumbling and a long face, Juliet actually likes being useful. She may want to get paid for certain tasks and why not? It is a way to provide her with extra pocket money which can be an incentive to save up for special acquisitions. For the purchase of major items (for example, a bicycle) you could pay half, once Juliet has saved half herself. She is far more likely to want and care for a possession that has involved such effort on her part and she'll learn to value money at an early age.

Time management is another important skill that you can model by working together to schedule her tasks for the coming week. Set a regular time for this — perhaps when she receives her pocket money, but allow the schedule to be flexible to cope with unexpected events.

Part 2

From Childhood to Maturity

A TIME OF TRANSITION

WHAT HAS HAPPENED TO JULIET?

The little bundle in your arms with wispy hair and tiny, perfect fingers drew an overwhelming surge of tenderness and protectiveness from you. How and when did that sweet baby turn into this angry adolescent girl whose behaviour makes you grind your teeth with frustration and despair?

YOU AND YOUR ADOLESCENT DAUGHTER

Your daughter will be well on her way to adolescence by the age of twelve. She knows a great deal about you, but you will be living with a chameleon. Just as you have adjusted to one development and think you have her figured out, she changes again.

Remember your own adolescence — unfamiliar body, unpredictable moods and undefined yearnings? Remember the fights with your parents when they treated you as a child but demanded you behave like an adult? The rites of passage were often as exhilarating and stomach-churning as a roller-coaster ride.

Now your daughter faces exactly the same confusion and struggle for self-knowledge as you did. The transition from child to adult is a tough one, particularly if you, as a loving and concerned parent, are determined to control the process and the outcome.

You can help her or make it harder. Your role as parent is to teach your daughter life skills which will guide her through the minefields ahead. Even though she is on the threshold of adulthood and your relationship is changing, *you* remain her parent. She looks to you for security, consistency and guidance. It is not your role to be a competitive mother or to be her pal. She will find pals among her own age group.

Adolescence is often a war of independence. You can win battles, but finally she must win the war.

IMPORTANT POINTS

- Spend exclusive time with your daughter, giving her your undivided attention. Chat while doing dishes together. Go out together for coffee or fruit juice — she will enjoy it as a 'grown-up' outing. You don't always have to spend money, try going to a quiet park with a thermos flask. It's important to make a relaxed time for her and you to spend together.
- Share jokes, exchange gossip, relate family anecdotes and laugh at mistakes. Be positive with her so that she sees you as a relaxed, outgoing person — not just the tense, serious parent.
- Have family meals together (without the TV blaring). Involve everyone in helping to set the table, pick flowers and serve food. Don't use mealtime to settle scores — it spoils the occasion. Teach your daughter to cook *her* favourite dishes. Adolescent friends love being invited to impromptu meals and on such informal occasions 'hard' topics such as drugs, alcoholism and contraception may crop up spontaneously in discussion.

- Children copy their parents and adults they admire. Good manners, confidence, poise and consideration for others are developed at home.
- Don't criticise your daughter continually. If your exchanges are limited to her shortcomings, you are reacting only to misbehaviour. Speak to your partner about alternative ways of managing unacceptable behaviour.
- Compliment your daughter for a job well done, for persevering with an unpleasant task, for showing self-control, for taking the trouble to look great. Draw attention to accomplishments: success at school, work, sport, etc. Praise her for good behaviour and performance. Acknowledge thoughtfulness. Don't take it for granted or, even worse, simply dismiss it as 'about time you showed *me* some consideration'.
- Treat your daughter with respect. Adolescents are reasonable beings... sometimes! Adults can be bloody-minded too. Let her know if you are under pressure and ask for her understanding. In return extend the same to her. You can't always be the perfect parent and she mustn't expect it. Teach by example. She will appreciate the courtesy of an apology.
- Mothers know how fragile and tired they get before a period, so they can sympathise with their daughter's premenstrual tension, stomach cramps and headaches. Remind other family members to 'ease off' at this time.
- Pressure from school commitments may also put your daughter under stress. Assignments, homework, extracurricular activities and parental expectations put conscientious students under enormous pressure. Does your daughter need to reassess her commitments?
- Loss of employment, parental conflict or moving house cause serious stress in families. Adolescents react badly, often unaware of the cause. Death or illness of a family member, of a friend or of household pets can be devastating too. If this has happened, make allowances.
- Don't overburden your daughter with domestic chores. Is she expected to do more than a boy just because she is a girl?

- Encourage your daughter to think for herself and take responsibility for her own actions. **You cannot make decisions for her forever**. With a little guidance from you, allow her to make decisions when still young — it will build up her self-esteem and self-confidence and she will learn from her mistakes.

- Career/subject choices can be confusing. Get advice from the school counsellor and go to career nights. Assess your daughter's interests, strengths and weaknesses. Be flexible. Keep her options open because her interests may change. She may want to be a pop singer at thirteen, but by sixteen she will have moved on. Changing courses is not the end of the world. Don't try to decide *her* future for her.

- Comfort and reassure her when she is hurt, upset or disappointed. 'Toughening her up' teaches her that the world is callous and unresponsive to her needs. Confiding a problem helps her face the situation and put it in perspective. It is easy to assume that a girl who looks like an eighteen-year-old thinks and behaves like one, even though she's only fifteen.

- Teenagers live in a vastly different and more affluent world to the one in which you grew up. Of course, you cannot meet *all* her demands. If you don't have the money, or have doubts about a proposed purchase, tell her. Advertising is aimed at adolescents to part them from their (and your) money. Having an allowance teaches girls to be selective.

- Be sensitive to her material needs. Most teenagers are dependent on their parents for much longer than previous generations. Scholarships and grants are now far harder to get or are non-existent. Part-time jobs help teenagers learn the value of money, but today jobs for the young are harder to get and family budgets are often tight.

- When your daughter, intent on forging her own identity, rejects your values — *don't* panic. She is testing what you have taught her against values she has encountered in the wider world. When she is most critical of you is often when she most needs *you* to be understanding — while at the same time angrily accusing you of 'not understanding *anything*'.

FINDING HER PLACE IN THE WORLD

IDENTITY

Remember feeling oppressed, hemmed in, needing to burst out of the confines of home to get away and be by yourself? The world was beckoning. If you can remember this, you may understand your adolescent daughter much better.

Juliet's physical and psychological growth lead to an intense curiosity about the world outside the confines of the family home. She is curious about how other people live and behave, she wants to experience alternative lifestyles and experiment with different looks. Boys are on her mind even if they haven't arrived on your doorstep.

Your adolescent daughter wants her own identity and to do this she feels that she must end her previous close association with you. It is very painful for parents to learn that their young daughter now keeps secrets from them. She resorts to hurtful stratagems to keep parents at arm's length. Friends seem far more important than parents. There are long telephone conversations, loud music behind closed bedroom doors and hours spent locked in the bathroom.

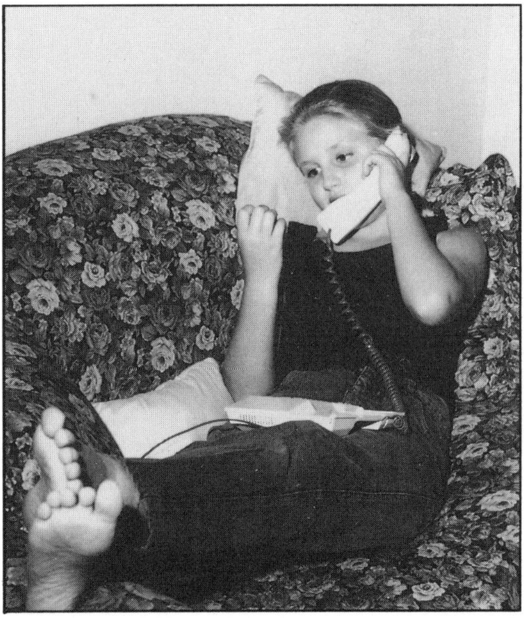

There may be dramatic changes in her appearance as she experiments with the 'latest' look: gelled or multi-coloured hair, haircuts that make you shudder, make-up and nail polish suitable for pantomime characters and what you consider totally outrageous clothes. Teenage fads you loathe, she will find irresistible.

'Don't you *trust* me?' is the disingenuous reproach

when you insist she be home by a reasonable hour, refuse her request to attend a party or sleep over at the house of people you don't know. And of course, you are the *only* parent with outdated ideas, such as ringing up to check whether there will be any adult supervision.

A major shift in the focus of your daughter's social and emotional life is occurring. This marks the beginning of a deliberate distancing from you — keeping you at a physical distance as well as emotionally separating from you. She wants to explore the world, discover where she fits into the scheme of things and establish her own identity. By now it becomes apparent that Nature's fiendish sense of humour often deliberately mismatches parents and daughters. Quiet, retiring parents are saddled with boisterous girls; fashion-conscious mothers with 'arty' daughters with dreadlocks; out-of-doors no-frills mothers with teenage fashion plates, keen to shop till they drop and acquire a gold credit card.

WILL THE MOTHER-DAUGHTER BOND SURVIVE?

Mother-daughter relations veer from the close and companionable to the confrontational, competitive and tense — they swivel from one extreme to the other with head-spinning rapidity.

Mum has been the most important person in Juliet's formative years and will remain the most influential. Hence the advice to suitors: 'Look at the mother to see what her daughter will become'.

Little boys go through a stage of wanting to marry their mothers; little girls go through a stage of wanting to *be* them. They play with dolls and toys, dress up in their mothers' clothes and are fascinated by the mystique of feminine garments, high heels, and perfume and by applying lipstick and eye make-up.

Many mothers find it difficult to come to terms with their adolescent daughters' struggle to find their own identities, particularly in cases when the mother was very close to her daughter during the early years. Boys start separating from their mothers around the age of six, when their interest shifts to the father or other male role models. A daughter's separation occurs during adolescence, when she focuses her emotional turmoil on her mother and expresses her rejection in searing criticism of many things her mother does. Girls' comments about their mothers' appearance, taste and personality can be exceedingly cruel. It may help to remember that adolescent girls are *just* as hard on themselves. Women, old and young, put a lot of pressure on themselves and their daughters to be perfect. Males tend to be more comfortable with themselves and less self-critical.

Adolescent girls in particular are curious about others' lives — their friends, other mothers, families and adults. They make comparisons, and their own mothers are certainly not exempted from their daughters' cool analysis. Try not to be crushed by wounding remarks. It can help to compare notes (in private) with other mothers who are enduring the same criticisms. No matter how attractive or popular, teenage girls are uncertain of themselves and look for reassurance. Sometimes *anything* you say will be misinterpreted and you cannot put a foot right. You may think she takes scant notice of your opinion, but you know her *better* than any of her friends and your comments will be taken to heart, although she may seem to ignore them.

Make time for her and be alert to her needs in what is, after all, a transitionary stage in her development. As she gets older and more mature, you will find that the bond between you will strengthen again. She has every reason to trust you and will consult you when she has a family of her own. When you feel low, remember that daughters can be a source of comfort in your middle years and old age.

IS DAD STILL HER HERO?

The relationship between father and daughter is different. There is that all-too-brief period when Dad is godlike and can do no wrong. He is the person on whom she practises charm and the gentle art of persuasion. Her first knowledge about men is acquired by spending time with him. She learns about trust and safety by doing things with him and learning from him.

When his daughter enters adolescence, Dad becomes even more protective of her than before, regarding other males as potential predators, heartbreakers and cads who could misuse her. When she begins to be interested in boys, Dad's feelings about this may be tinged with resentment and jealousy. But she needs his reassurance when her romance founders. It is Dad who reassures her that she is irresistible in spite of her spots, braces on her teeth and freckles.

There are bleak periods when she regards her father as an ignorant, insensitive old duffer. Dad may never be her hero again, but, hopefully, she will eventually recognise his good intentions and devotion and be grateful for his loving care.

ROLE OF FRIENDS

Your friends are an important source of support, companionship and social contact for you and your family. They are sometimes closer and more understanding than relatives and, when relatives are far away, they can assume their roles. Close friends have the potential to be seen as role models by your children and can be called upon for assistance, if the need arises. They are not caught up in the emotional turmoil which often exists in families, but they are sufficiently close, loved and trusted to be consulted if necessary.

Being invited to stay with close family friends for a few days is often a welcome change for the adolescent, who feels she is away from all that parental scrutiny and nagging. The parents also benefit from breathing space. The opportunity to discuss matters of interest with an adult (other than a parent or teacher) is usually welcomed by teenagers, who, in doing so, feel accepted and 'grown up'. It is amazing how much more 'adult' daughters seem when they have been away from home for a week or two with friends and experienced life in another household.

Through your daughter you will meet other parents, teachers and coaches at school, sporting and social functions. Get to know the parents of your daughter's friends and discuss issues of concern with them. Teenagers have a wonderful way of isolating you as the sole freakish parent who is unreasonable about curfews, going out alone, clothes, pocket money, etc. Don't you remember pulling that one on *your* parents?

You can nurture the capacity for friendship in your daughter:

- **By accepting and encouraging her early friendships.**
- **By inviting her friends for impromptu meals and sleep-overs or taking them on excursions or holidays.**
- **By allowing her to accept invitations to friends' homes whose parents you have met (but check by telephone she really *is* there).**
- **By being tolerant and recognising your daughter's need to move outside the protective home environment, in order to learn about other people and how they live.**

It is important to keep in contact with relatives and share family occasions. Cousins make good friends for life. Remind her to send cards and notes to relatives on birthdays and other occasions. A beneficial friendship can be formed with a friend or relative who falls midway between the age of your daughter and you. Such a friend can be an important influence, someone your daughter can confide in over topics which secretly worry most girls, such as problems about attracting boys or gender confusions. Some girls would rather *die* than discuss such subjects with their mothers.

Such supportive relationships — including those with childless aunts or godmothers — can prove a source of strength and comfort on both sides. Don't feel threatened if your daughter develops a friendship like this with an older woman.

Oil painting by Marie Laurencin. Private collection

APPLYING RULES AND SETTING BOUNDARIES

Ground rules are there for good reasons. The most important consideration is your daughter's *safety* and your peace of mind. Your daughter should also learn to have respect for other people and their property.

While the need for rules is obvious to parents, teenagers often regard them as unfair attempts to limit their freedom. If your daughter understands and accepts the reason for a certain rule, a cause of potential conflict is removed. Unfortunately, most teenagers regard themselves as adults, confidently tackling the world, while caring parents are keenly aware of potential dangers.

Rules are more likely to be observed when they are mutually agreed. If your daughter is particularly wilful, her acceptance of ground or house rules will make it easier for all concerned. Keep discussions constructive. Encourage her to negotiate if she wants a change to a particular rule. Learning how to get changes by negotiation rather than by confrontation is an important life skill which will help her all her life.

Draw up rules which are appropriate for your daughter's age and commitments and modify them as she gets older. Check with parents of your daughter's friends to find out what arrangements they have arrived at, if you are uncertain.

Be flexible. Take into consideration that times have changed since *you* were a teenager. Students are often expected to take part in extracurricular activities, organised by various groups. Before the beginning of the new school year, find out how these may affect her study time. Also consider her safety, if public transport has to be used for such activities.

Disagreement between parents on points of discipline or rules will encourage your daughter to shop around for the decision she wants. Resist her attempts to wangle a favourable decision by playing one parent off against the other. Being seen as 'twisted around his daughter's little finger' and 'a soft touch' could lead to great discomfort for Dad and could have repercussions.

Check with your partner if you have any doubts about a particular request. Involve the other partner in important discussions with your daughter, but if possible, refrain from contradicting or overriding each other in front of her.

WHEN RULES ARE BROKEN

Juliet can give you a hard time by simply ignoring previously negotiated house rules when it suits her. Punishment rarely works, so is there any point in making rules if she doesn't adhere to them?

Rules have been broken before: it is *not* the end of the world. Don't let the situation get out of hand — call a temporary retreat to allow tempers to cool and back off with dignity. Use a cooling-off period to reassess the situation in a less heated fashion. Listen to your daughter, find out *why* she objects, then negotiate a solution. *Your* experience and understanding of your daughter should provide some insight into her behaviour.

Joining a parents' support group may help. You will become aware of the fact that other parents are going through similar ordeals — they may be able to offer constructive solutions to your particular problems with broken rules. As a last resort, you may look for professional advice. Counselling helps, but if that fails too, you may find yourself in a deadlock situation.

You have gone through adolescence yourself; you know it's only a temporary state, so try to keep things in perspective. Remember, most unruly individuals grow up to be responsible adults. That prospect may be of some comfort to you when Juliet's teenage obstinacy is getting you down. Many risk-taking teenagers give their parents sleepless nights. Only a few suffer the consequences of their reckless behaviour and pay dearly, sometimes with their lives. Adolescents learn eventually that they *must* live with the consequences of their own actions.

CURFEWS AND RESPONSIBILITIES

It is one thing to impose late night curfews on your daughter, but making her observe them is another matter. Up to the age of fifteen, you may still have control by applying penalties (for example, grounding her, withholding pocket money, not allowing her to watch television, etc). But beyond that age, some teenagers are openly defiant and penalties become increasingly ineffectual.

Talking to her about potential dangers may not impress an adolescent who has no concept of her own vulnerability. Involve your daughter in drawing up basic rules, which should apply to all family members including parents. The following are suggested:

- **Always leave a contact name, address and phone number when going out in the evening (a whiteboard is handy for this).**
- **Phone home if she will be out after a nominated time, for instance after 6.00 pm or sunset — whichever comes earlier. Remember, phone cards are useful for this.**
- **Be sure Juliet has enough money for a taxi fare home and does not drive with anyone who has been drinking.**

SHARING RESPONSIBILITIES

The role of today's mothers has changed a great deal. Whatever the reason for returning to work — the desire to work for its own sake, family, professional obligations or financial need — what has *not* changed is the expectation that the mother will be the prime care-giver of the family. This often means that Mum has taken on an extra job without *any* reduction in family responsibilities.

While there is some concern about stress and fatigue among working mothers with very young children, this can be a positive situation for everyone, where older children are involved. Some adult supervision will be required up to their mid-teens. Depending on age, they can be expected to take on responsibility for looking after their own things and doing some of the chores. Knowing how to prepare a meal, do the laundry, iron one's clothes, tidy and clean her bedroom and the bathroom are essential steps towards adulthood and independent living.

Becoming responsible is not something that happens overnight; it is a maturation process beginning as early as preschool. Whether or not you have a job in addition to your family responsibilities, your daughter is quite capable of helping around the home. Unfortunately for mothers, it doesn't always work that way.

IS JULIET'S ROOM A PRIMAL CAVE?

You don't have to search for too long before coming across a teenage bedroom that resembles the lodging of a cave dweller. An academic recently announced that mothers should not worry about their daughter's untidiness — what mattered was that girls were raised to be loving and caring. Well, he was right, but only up to a point, and clearly couldn't have inspected many girls' bedrooms. In some girls' rooms one can scarcely *see* the bed for piles of clothes, damp and smelly towels, an assortment of discarded school socks, teen magazines and dirty coffee mugs. Painting materials, discarded school projects made from egg boxes, old boots and shoes and an empty bird cage sometimes add to the clutter.

If you don't teach your daughter the rudiments of housework and tidiness before she turns fourteen, you may as well hang up a sign '*Abandon hope all ye who enter here*'. You are likely to end up with a daughter incapable of throwing anything away or tidying up after herself.

Be forewarned. As soon as school studies get more intensive and exams loom, Juliet will give these as excuses for not cleaning up after her. 'Mucking out' her room will definitely *not* be a priority. Such excuses will continue throughout Grades 11 and 12 and, if still at home, on through university. One day she will in all probability leave the family home to share an apartment or house with others. What are the consequences if you have raised a 'sharer from hell'? — someone with whom no person, who actually *does* housework, wants to share. Charming, delightful and intelligent as she may be, she *won't* help with the washing-up and her room will resemble a rubbish tip or that primal cave, as it did before.

When Juliet eventually meets her Romeo, her hope of domestic happiness will hinge on whether he was raised by a Mum who taught him to be that rare gem, a male who will do the housework without complaining. A few trusting mothers believe that, when their daughter has to pay rent or a mortgage on a home of her own, she'll change fast enough. In the meantime they resign themselves to doing *all* the housework unaided. Other mothers put up with the situation for years, then finally snap and retaliate.

A Real-life Story

HOW ONE MOTHER DEALT WITH HER DAUGHTER'S UNTIDINESS

Tired of her teenage daughter's room resembling an archaeological site with layers of dirty clothes piled on top of each other, this particular mother threatened retaliation, but did nothing. The teenage daughter (who had a part-time job) claimed she was *far* too busy working in the local delicatessen to tidy up her room; yet, somehow she always had enough time to go to the cinema or out dancing.

Finally, after months of unsuccessful nagging, the mother had enough, realising she was being taken totally for granted. She walked into her daughter's room, gathered up all the dirty clothes lying in crumpled piles on the floor, loaded them in the car and took them to the dry-cleaners. When her daughter returned from school she found a neat, clean room. Thinking her mother had cleaned up and done her laundry as usual, she demanded, 'Where are my clothes, Mum?'

'At the dry-cleaners, dear', replied her mother calmly. 'They'll be back the day after tomorrow, all listed and in plastic bags. Your dresses and shirts will be on wire hangers for you to put in the wardrobe. From now on, anything I find lying around will be dry-cleaned. You'll have to pay to get your things back.'

The unusual strategy, born out of desperation, worked. The daughter learned the consequences of ignoring her mother's warnings. Her room is now relatively tidy and her clothes hang on wire hangers in her wardrobe.

Of course, this solution is only suitable with girls who have a substantial allowance or a part-time job. Beware of adopting this method, unless your daughter has **sufficient money to cover the dry-cleaning** — if not, you may find she is secretly sneaking money out of your purse to pay for the dry-cleaning.

GETTING YOUR DAUGHTER TO BECOME TIDY

Training your daughter to clear up after herself, do her *own* washing and ironing and learn to cook some simple dishes is essential for independent living. Apart from keeping the family home habitable, doing the chores alongside your daughter can have another spin-off. While you are both working side by side on dull and routine chores, something that is bothering her may emerge quite naturally in conversation and can be discussed.

We questioned several parents to find out how they managed to get their teenage daughters to help with housework. The following strategies emerged:

1 **Mothers who gave in and did it themselves:** About one in every three mothers admitted they had failed — these mothers cleaned their daughters' rooms, washed and ironed their clothes. Some selfless souls even washed the boyfriends' shirts after they had been allowed to become household fixtures.

2 **Mothers who gave in and engaged a cleaner:** You may be affluent and lucky enough to have a cleaner once or twice a week, but it is amazing how quickly an untidy person can create chaos around her.

3 **Retribution — the culprits pay: first version of 'learning through consequences'**. At a family conference Mum announced that there was only so much money in the household budget. Because the children wouldn't clean up, a cleaning agency would be employed at the rate of $15.00 upwards per hour. *They* would lose out as under this arrangement there wouldn't be the money for that trip to xxx or that CD player or whatever the children wanted so badly.

4 **Retribution — the culprits pay: second version:** If kids have a part-time job, which they insist stops them helping out at home, they each contribute 20% of their earnings to paying a cleaning agency.

5 **Buy-back scheme:** One mother decided to confiscate all personal items littering the house and lock them away. She told her daughters they could buy them back at 50 cents an item, the total to be deducted from their weekly pocket money.

6 **Duty rosters:** Optimistic mothers organise rotas, using a whiteboard or computerised list with everyone's jobs clearly outlined on it. Scheduling Saturday mornings works best.

Duty roster	November															
Job	1	2	3	4	5	6	7	8	9	10	11	12	13	14	15	1
Juliet																
Set dinner table	✓	✓														
Stack dishwasher	✓	✓														
Tidy up your room	✓															
Mary																
Clear dinner table	✓	✓														
Empty dishwasher	✓															
Tidy up your room	✓	✓														
John																
Walk the dog	✓	✓														
Vacuum clean	✓															
Take garbage out	✓	✓														

7 **Bribery:** Motivate your kids through a scheme, similar to 'Fly Buys' or other travel incentives. As a reward for doing various household jobs, points are allocated to each child. A certain sum of points earns a treat, such as an outing, an interstate flight to see a relative or friend, or financial assistance towards buying a bicycle. Yes, of course it's a mild form of bribery, but so are most travel incentive schemes.

ARE YOU READY TO LOOSEN THE REINS?

As she grows older Juliet will spend more and more time away from home and be exposed to temptations and dangers that give you nightmares. She will start secondary school, travel by public transport where she will meet boys, later she will want to go out at night to a disco or cinema with a boy. With your permission, she will stay overnight at girlfriends' homes.

You are filled with anxiety and believe that things will go dreadfully wrong, unless you keep a close eye on everything your daughter does. This means you can't come to terms with your diminished role in her life. But in many things you *have* to trust her, even more so as she gets older. If you want to build a mature relationship with her, be prepared to forgive mistakes and hope she *learns* from them. So don't hold on too tight to the reins — if you do, sooner or later you may lose control and the horse will bolt.

THE LEARNING PROCESS

KNOWLEDGE IS POWER

Knowledge is the key to understanding ourselves and our world. The learning process includes formal and informal learning: both are important and independent of each other.

Formal learning occurs in schools and the workplace. Juliet learns about the nature of our world and how its various institutions work. She learns to read, write and reason; how to retrieve information and other essential skills needed in a technological society. She prepares herself for a career of her choice and for integration into the wider community.

Informal learning is what your daughter acquires through life experiences and the socialising process she gets from family, relatives, friends, neighbours and peer groups.

Both processes teach her what kind of behaviour is appropriate under certain circumstances and with particular groups of people — the family, in the classroom, in the workplace, at playing sport, at job interviews, etc.

Girls must learn about responsibilities, self-discipline and privileges, about making choices and commitment and how to accept the consequences of their actions. Your pre-teen daughter, so full of promise and anticipation, has already absorbed much essential information — how well she handles the coming years of transition will depend on how prepared both of you are.

RAISING HER SELF-ESTEEM

Self-esteem means feeling good about yourself, comfortable with your appearance and who you are, confident in your ability to do things well and able to get on well with others. Self-esteem is *not* arrogance, it is self-respect. Arrogance is disrespect for the feelings and rights of others.

Low self-esteem causes adolescents to behave obnoxiously. Under their bravado and defiance they are *vulnerable* because they are young and inexperienced, they are *anxious* because they don't want to look foolish and *confused* as so many things are happening all at once in their lives.

HOW *YOU* CAN HELP

STRATEGIES FOR RAISING SELF-ESTEEM

- **Emphasise her strengths**. Be reassuring and confident about her ability to work out problems.
- **Build up her confidence**. Give her experience in doing things, such as making appointments over the telephone. Support her when she is uncertain. Compliment her on achievements, appearance, behaviour — anything about her that you like.
- **Plan ahead**. Around birthdays or the New Year, review the events of the past year and ask her what changes she anticipates, like a new school, transport, new activities, work. Discuss her commitments with her and set priorities jointly.
- **Listen to her when she wants to talk**. Twelve months makes a big difference physically, emotionally and mentally, in her young life. Tune in to *her* feelings. Ask *her* opinion. Encourage her to reason with you. Don't let her storm off complaining 'What's the use? You *never* listen to me!'
- **Build a sense of competence**. She may be able to make sense of the instructions accompanying electronic equipment! Being able to do and make things builds a sense of competence. Being able to cook, for example, gives pleasure and is a survival skill.
- **Encourage independence**. Involve her in decisions concerning her own life. Handling money is a necessary life skill: an allowance can include components to cover expenses such as fares, presents, clothes, as well as discretionary spending. Encourage her to take responsibility, step by step, for her own ironing, school lunches and occasional evening meals.
- **Transfer responsibility**. Being late, missing deadlines, losing or forgetting things is *her* responsibility, not yours.

Your relationship with your daughter and your parenting style will have an enormous amount to do with the way she makes the transition to adulthood.[1] The way you have brought her up and the methods you have used will have a bearing on her self-confidence, on the way she deals with situations, as well as on the kind of relationship you have during this time and into the future.

YOUR INVOLVEMENT WITH JULIET'S FORMAL EDUCATION

Because school takes up at least six hours a day, five days a week, it has a substantial influence on your daughter and plays a critical role in her intellectual, emotional and social development. For all these reasons you should be involved in her schooling. Get to know her teachers; let nothing prevent you from attending parent/teacher evenings; if possible, become involved in school life.

Go to school concerts and plays; take time off to work in the tuckshop or bookshop; attend open days and information evenings; join Parents & Friends Associations or similar parent groups. You will learn how your daughter is getting on with her subjects, classmates and school life in general and you will have early warning if something is wrong. You will also meet parents facing similar difficulties. Schools are political places and a parent who is involved is a force to be reckoned with. It doesn't matter what school your daughter attends, your input is important for her development.

MOTIVATING JULIET TO STUDY

'Lacks motivation, could do better' on report cards makes some parents see red, while others despair. A small minority of students know what they want to do and are very focused: Theirs are the lucky parents!

For the majority of students, having a goal is the most important factor affecting their motivation. Parental support and the home environment come next.

Recognise Juliet's abilities and interests and put these ahead of your own aims for her. Whatever they are — academic, creative, musical, organisational, financial — encourage her to develop these talents. Your support will encourage her to explore *her* potential.

If she doesn't know which course is right for her (or lacks interest in anything in particular) you could start by selecting a course which matches her ability.[2] She may need to try a number of options before she decides what she wants. Today's students are expected to make choices when they are fifteen, a time when many have no clear idea of what they want to do. Your daughter may need more life experience. Enrolling in a course and changing her mind is not a mistake — view it as a learning experience.

AT THE PIANO. Auguste Renoir. Musée du Louvre, Paris.

Sarah was gifted musically and dreamt of a singing career. She studied piano theory and practice, took singing lessons, classes in classical ballet, jazz ballet. In Years 11 and 12 she selected music and drama as her elective subjects.

Her parents had serious misgivings about Sarah closing her options and feared she would spend most of her life waitressing while her voice matured and her breaks came. They met with the school guidance counsellor, who advised that it would be a mistake to insist that Sarah do subjects other than those she saw as relevant. He stressed the importance of motivation in a student's attitude.

After much soul-searching the parents accepted Sarah's choices. She obtained excellent results in Year 12 but, by that time, had decided against a stage career. She went to university, changed courses twice in her first year before she found that what she really wanted was to study medicine. Sarah then enrolled in night classes to do additional Year 11 and 12 subjects she needed in order to reach her goal and practise medicine.

Having a goal gives direction, while motivation strengthens the resolve to continue when friends, warm weather and temptation beckon. Why do students of migrant families often outperform other students? It is not just that the migrant parents value education, or recognise it as the key to a better life; the students themselves are motivated to succeed.

Education does not necessarily take place just in colleges and universities. Your daughter's interests should influence the choice of courses and institutions. Be flexible and be informed. Many of the jobs previously available in banking, the public sector, the railways, etc., are no longer there, due to the revolution in information technology.

The very best start you can give your daughter is by providing a rich and stimulating environment from infancy. Television is part of our lives but should not be an important part of your child's developing years. There are other far more important things to experience.

POINTS TO REMEMBER

- Expose Juliet to music by learning an instrument, or joining a school or church choir. Take her to concerts and musicals, if this is possible. Encourage her to view music as something that enriches life, now and in the future.
- Explore museums, zoos and botanic gardens with her.
- Encourage her to draw or do pottery. Most children will enjoy visiting a public art gallery (in most cases free of charge), provided the visit does not last longer than an hour. Buy Juliet a postcard of her 'favourite' painting in the bookshop and, afterwards, have a drink and a cake with her in the coffee shop. When she gets older, increase the length of the visits.
- Teach her to respect and love national parks, the birds and animals in them and go there on family excursions.
- Enrol her in your local public library to foster a love of reading.

WHAT SCHOOL?

Some parents follow family tradition in choice of school; others base their choice on their daughter's preference, abilities and interests and the reputation of the school.

Single-sex schools versus co-ed schools: Opinion is divided, but data suggest that girls do better at single-sex schools for a variety of reasons. Girls are ahead of boys in maturity, social development and language skills. Incidents of sexual harassment and bullying by boys have been reported. On the other hand, in later years some subjects such as English Literature are more interesting in a mixed class. A co-ed school is more representative of our community.

Private versus government: Fees payable at private schools vary greatly depending on the school, the city it is located in and its religious affiliation (Catholic schools tend to have lower fees). Education at government or public schools is not free, as books have to be bought and certain charges are imposed.

Academic versus skill-based schools: You are setting Juliet up for failure and unhappiness if you try to force her to enter an edu-

cational stream she is neither equipped for nor interested in. A skill-based school or training college could be a better choice for her.

Day girl versus boarder: Living in an isolated area as well as family tradition may lead to a decision to board. Families in crisis and parents whose work involves frequent relocations or overseas postings often opt for boarding schools.

School uniforms: The heat seems to have gone out of the discussion about uniform versus non-uniform schools. The dress code is more relaxed at government schools than at private schools, most of which maintain a strict policy on students wearing uniforms.

SUBJECT CHOICES/CAREER DECISIONS

Your daughter is one of the lucky few if she has a clear idea of what career she wants when it's time to choose her subjects. The nagging fear about making the wrong choice is twofold: the career may be less satisfying than she expected or opportunities in it may be scarce or no longer available. School counsellors are a valuable source of information on career prospects and on your daughter's potential.

It is advisable, as stated previously, to let your daughter choose a course and subjects she enjoys. There is no way you can force her to learn something she dislikes or for which she has absolutely no aptitude. There is always the chance that your daughter's interests will change. Night classes are offered in most secondary school subjects, so that it is possible to pick up a subject which was not studied at school or for which better grades are required. Motivation is the key to success. Very often older or mature-age students tend to achieve excellent grades once they come to value learning.

A minority of students are academic, another minority don't fit the mainstream. Forcing a student to undertake an inappropriate course is destined to cause harm, not the least of which is loss of confidence, hatred of learning, resentment and problem behaviour. Forcing your daughter to stay on at school for longer than she is willing, often done with the highest of motives 'for her own good', rarely achieves desired results. Listen to your daughter, get career advice and accept if a conventional career path doesn't suit her.

HOMEWORK AND DIFFICULTIES AT SCHOOL

Your role in supervising homework and assignments should be negligible during high school. Although you may have to encourage your daughter to do her homework, it won't help to tie her down to her chair! The unpleasant consequence of *not* doing homework is one lesson she must learn herself.

If she is having difficulty with homework, this must be brought to the attention of her teachers, so that the problem can be addressed through additional tuition, explanation of guidelines, extension of deadlines, etc. Be alert for changes in your daughter's behaviour — withdrawal, introversion, tearfulness — that cannot be accounted for by the moodiness to which teenagers are normally prone. The change may be caused by unhappiness at school — a problem with a teacher, a disciplinary matter, a difficult assignment or even a quarrel with a friend.

Most teachers derive great personal satisfaction from seeing their students develop and succeed. Only a small minority today strike terror in the classroom. *Any* teacher who uses intimidation, verbal abuse and humiliation is a bully. If you feel you have grounds for concern, you should list them, then contact the school's principal or a school counsellor (if the school has one), and express your concerns to them.

HOW *you* CAN HELP

- Make sure Juliet has a quiet place to do her homework without interference from the TV or other siblings. A study area with enough desk space and shelving would be ideal.
- Ensure homework has *priority* over other activities.
- Don't act as your daughter's research assistant for her assignments. Time management and carrying out research is all part of the learning process and assessment by the teacher.
- Don't substantially correct or rewrite her assignments. Her teacher is monitoring your daughter's progress and problems. Helping your daughter with 'take-home' exams is *cheating*.
- If your daughter has difficulties with school, speak *calmly* to her class teacher or house mistress if it is a general problem; her subject teacher, school counsellor or guidance officer if it concerns a particular subject area. Tell them if there are difficulties at home (for example, death, illness, separation, divorce, unemployment or financial problems), as any of these factors can adversely affect your daughter's school work and behaviour.
- If she has behavioural or developmental problems or is generally unhappy at school, contact her class teacher or school counsellor. If you remain unsatisfied, contact the principal or the deputy.

MANAGING MONEY

Learning to manage money is one of life's daunting tasks. Part of the trick of being a successful parent is to allow your daughter, as soon as possible, to take control of her own finances.[3]

For teenage girls, clothes and grooming products are an expensive and contentious matter. Consider including a modest clothes component in your daughter's allowance — it will teach her to be selective, encourages her to shop more sensibly and plan ahead to take advantage of sales. Most girls become fairly canny about spending their 'own' money. Be specific about items that are not included in her allowance. She will certainly appreciate your offer to buy or contribute to the cost of an item you both like.

HER FIRST 'FORMAL' DANCE

There are a number of milestones for your daughter to look forward to in Year 12 — the end of school is in sight. In the following months your daughter will put thoughts of final exams, assignments and decisions about the future into the background and focus on planning for the dinner-dance known in Australia as 'The Formal'. Exclusive private schools and local country high schools now hold the equivalent of what was once the 'silvertail' or debutante set's 'coming-out ball'. Some of these rite-of-passage dances are organised by the schools themselves and some by the students.

DANCE IN THE CITY
Oil painting by Auguste Renoir
Musée d'Orsay, Paris

It is possible for your daughter to be well-groomed and beautifully dressed without you becoming bankrupt. Most schools encourage the selection of venues which are reasonably priced. It is the extras which can blow the budget. Set a limit and have her list and price the things she needs:

- **tickets for herself and escort (if from another school),**
- **buttonhole for escort,**
- **hairdressing appointment,**
- **purchases of make-up, nail polish, stockings, shoes,**
- **undergarments and accessories, and importantly,**
- **the dress.**

Your daughter has probably been collecting pictures of outfits for some months. Try to look round shops with her to see what is available within her budget, noting styles and colours which suit her figure. If necessary, steer her away from slinky black dresses, plunge necklines and teetering heels (which she may feel spell sophistication) into a more classical look. She can take advantage of sales only if she knows what she wants. When deciding on the dress and accessories, remind her that she will attend other functions in the future, so it is sensible to buy things which can be used later.

Finally, be cautious about pre-dance drink parties (or parties after the dance) held at the homes of school friends. Most schools discourage drinking before the dance because in the past some students have arrived intoxicated. To avoid this, some schools now hold their own pre-formal parties, to which parents are invited.

HER FIRST HOLIDAY WITHOUT PARENTS

This is something many parents dread, especially in Queensland and New South Wales and other coastal resorts round Australia, where an end-of-school celebration (a rite of passage known as 'Schoolies') takes place. At this time landlords of run-down holiday apartments make a mint letting them out to school-leavers, hell bent on celebrating the end of school. Of considerable concern to parents during such holidays are excessive alcohol consumption, drug use and sex — perils that are discussed elsewhere in this book.

Following horror stories of drunkenness and violence on Queensland's Gold Coast, local authorities, police, the business community and residents tackled the problem of vandalism and drunken rampages and developed a strategy to head off antisocial behaviour. They provided activities and venues for teenagers to let off steam, and celebrate in more socially acceptable ways. Now many beach resorts, which once banned school-leavers holidaying without parents, welcome them during that otherwise quiet period in Australia just before Christmas.

Your concern about *any* first holiday involving a group of teens without adult supervision is understandable. This is the first *serious* test of your daughter's common sense, maturity and ability to say 'NO', just as it will be if she goes overseas alone. Warn her firmly against the perils of hitch-hiking. If possible, make sure you know *where* she will be staying and have a contact phone number for her in case of emergencies. For your *own* peace of mind, agree to accept collect calls or assist her to get a mobile phone, so that frequent contact can take place during the period she is away.

ONCE YOUR DAUGHTER GETS HER DRIVER'S LICENCE

Having a driving licence *and* the use of a car are important milestones for any teenager. However, adolescence and cars make a potentially dangerous mix. Cars have become more powerful — old bangers can be dangerous while young drivers are still inexperienced and unfamiliar with routes and with the effects of alcohol.

Joy rides are not uncommon, involving high-speed races, dangerous driving and dares. Alcohol and recreational drugs only magnify these risks. *Not* getting into a car with other adolescents under these conditions, saying 'I'm sorry, but no' to friends and acquaintances after a party and *resisting* peer pressure require a cool head and strength of character on the part of your daughter.

Motoring organisations advise against giving a newly licensed driver a powerful car. Girls tend to be more cautious drivers than boys, but this doesn't safeguard them from the risk of being involved in traffic accidents. Once your daughter has her driving licence, you may allow her to use the family car from time to time. However, you must negotiate consistent rules as to who pays for the petrol and when and for how long she can use it, otherwise you may find yourself subsidising her *and* her friends, and without transport just when *you* need it!

All teenagers should be encouraged to attend defensive driving courses. Acquiring adequate driving skills and being able to cope with the unexpected are worthwhile insurances for your daughter's safety.

BECOMING SEXUALLY MATURE

HORMONES, PUBERTY 'BLUES' AND ROLE MODELS

Hormones — those biochemical time bombs which trigger behavioural and physical changes — have the capacity to leave your daughter and everyone in her vicinity in turmoil.

Your daughter will yell, 'Stop treating me like a child!', telling you that *your* method of dealing with her is out of step with *her* perceptions of maturity. Teenage rebellion as depicted in the tabloids shows drug offenders in juvenile courts, obsessed with sex, drugs and loud music. In reality most teenagers *aren't* like that. They are idealistic and keen to 'save planet earth', although many enjoy loud music and this is the period in their lives when they are most worried about sex and their own appeal. The influence of 1960s feminists has irrevocably changed men's perception of women and women's perception of themselves. However, girls today find the portrayal of women in film and pop culture of the 1960s hilarious. Feminists' achievements are taken for granted in the post-feminist era. Most young women now refuse to call themselves feminists.

EVE. Wood engraving by Eric Gill.
Private collection.

With whom do today's girls identify? Not with the feminists of the 1960s, nor with the superwomen of the 1980s like Margaret Thatcher, Golda Meier and Indira Gandhi, who were then key players on an international stage. They have no equivalent today.

Who are seen by our popular press as female role models or significant women? Kylie Minogue, Naomi Campbell, Demi Moore, Julia Roberts and the

Spice Girls are the stars of contemporary women's magazines and teen publications. The 1990s saw the emergence of supermodels as role models. For many girls they have become the epitome of the unattainable. Their physique — height, slenderness and long legs — redefined the concept of feminine beauty. Should the superficial worlds of Hollywood and fashion modelling, where most actresses and models are commodities with a short shelf-life, provide us with role models for impressionable girls? Why don't women's magazines run stories on courageous women, like those young female doctors who devote their lives to working in fistula or leprosy clinics and children's hospitals in the Third World?

Inspiring role models

There are excellent role models in the professions, commerce and sport as well as inspiring women with impact on our cultural and political scene, who remain largely unknown to adolescents. For this reason Susanna de Vries wrote *Strength of Purpose,* containing biographies of the first Australian and British women to overcome discrimination and enter male-dominated enclaves such as law, medicine, politics and Olympic sports.[1] Unfortunately, today's tabloids and women's magazines are filled with stories about drug-addicted pop stars and partners, who attempt suicide with depressing frequency, or lavish-spending younger female members of various Royal households whose names are linked with many different men. No one wants to return to Enid Blyton-type characters in books and magazines, but are women so obviously addicted to pleasure and narcissism inspiring role models for young girls?

Lack of good role models or any belief system contribute, to what some psychologists and teachers now define as 'spiritual anorexia'. This term means a depressive wasting-away of the spirit and bleak nihilism. Girls from broken or abusive homes, who lack a positive belief system or family support, are at risk from spiritual anorexia. In some cases such circumstances have caused depressive illness or even suicide. Other factors which may lead to spiritual anorexia include prolonged exposure to life-cheapening values such as the glorification of casual sex, gross materialism and a profound belief that it is impossible to save the world from pollution or destruction. We must see girls receive positive messages and good role models to counteract this nihilistic approach to life.

BEHAVIOURAL CHANGES

All those hormones, including oestrogen, coursing through your daughter's developing body produce more than breasts, hips and pubic hair. They bring pimples, moodiness, tears and defiance. Try to remember what you were like at that age. A model teenager? Reasonable? Responsible? Really? Think again. The teenage years are a period of turbulent conflict with parents, teachers and anyone *else* who tries to set limits to adolescent lives. Behavioural changes include argumentativeness, defiance, disregard of curfews, impatience, irritability and sheer bloody-mindedness — characteristics many adults *also* exhibit!

Unfortunately, when the physical changes are most obvious and behaviour is most challenging, emotional growth is not in step. Emotional maturity develops more gradually and unevenly; hence parents' complaints about the infantile behaviour of adult-looking teenagers. The girl who *looks* like a young woman is still a *child* in many ways. And can be, at times, a moody, irrational child.

Teenagers demand more independence and freedom from parental restrictions. 'Don't you *trust* me?' is the less-than-candid reproach when you insist they be home by a reasonable hour or refuse their request to attend an all-night party or sleep-over at the home of people you don't know. And, of course, you are the only parent with such outdated ideas as ringing up to check whether there will be adult supervision.

A major shift in the focus of your daughter's social and emotional life has occurred. It marks the beginning of a deliberate psychological and emotional separation from you while she explores the outside world, discovers who she is and where she fits into the general scheme of things.

DIET AND THE IMPORTANCE OF BALANCE

A balanced diet will prevent some of the problems common to this age. But good eating habits don't occur overnight, so establishing positive attitudes at an early age to food and good eating habits is essential. You yourself provide her with an example, good or bad.

Our body shape is as much the result of genes as the food we eat. Putting on weight during adolescence is normal, with gains in height and body circumference. Gaining weight is not the greatest harm we can inflict on ourselves — being significantly underweight has more serious consequences (see Eating Disorders).

Teeth, skin, nails and hair — the focus of girls' obsession — are indications of health and nutrition. If you want to establish good eating habits, don't make mealtime the occasion for family rows. It doesn't help anyone's digestion or advance family relationships. Meals should be enjoyable occasions rather than confrontational. Good ingredients, simply prepared and attractively served in a warm, affectionate environment, do much to build positive attitudes to healthy living, food and family.

PHYSICAL ACTIVITY

Most schools provide an extensive program of physical activities which are designed to cater for a range of interests and abilities. Whether these activities are of a competitive or a social nature, all girls are expected to participate as part of the school's curriculum and a way of building muscular coordination. When your daughter plays sport, make sure she wears a properly fitted mouthguard. The consequences of a direct hit to the mouth are devastating as well as expensive.

Unfortunately, when they leave school, many girls stop playing sport, reduce physical activity, put on weight and commence crash dieting. Luckily, dancing is an excellent form of exercise and energetic dances are the rage. Partners are optional.

ACNE — A HORMONAL HORROR

Acne is triggered by hormones (including testosterone — yes, even girls have it) going into overdrive producing far too much oil in the glands which, in turn, plugs up the pores and turns to pimples or blackheads. Between 60% and 80% of teenagers will get acne, 15% severely. Acne is not caused by rich or fatty foods, though they don't exactly help. Neither is it due to poor personal hygiene. Acne is a fact of life for teenagers everywhere. You should reassure your daughter that this is only a temporary phase. A wide range of acne zappers are on sale at all chemists because treating acne has become big business. Acne in some teenagers can lead to facial scarring so, if you are worried, your daughter should see her family doctor, who will recommend appropriate treatment. Very severe cases of acne should always be referred to a skin specialist.

HOW *you* CAN HELP

TO MINIMISE YOUR DAUGHTER'S ACNE AND PERSONAL HYGIENE PROBLEMS

ADVISE HER:

- To ensure her diet contains plenty of fruit, vegetables, protein and carbohydrates, which are the foundation of good health.
- To drink at least six glasses of water a day to flush away unwanted toxins and replace all those fizzy drinks, whenever possible, in favour of water or pure fruit juice.
- To shower or bathe frequently because increased sweat glands and teenage anxieties will make her perspire far more than previously. Without a good deodorant, such heavy perspiration will cause body odour.
- Not to *squeeze* those blackheads, zits or whatever. They reappear and can cause scars. What is important is to cure the overproduction of oil, the source of the infection.
- To use a foaming medicated skin and pore wash, obtainable from chemists, to control mild cases of acne, although this is not the solution for really bad cases. Morning cleansing is vital, as we all tend to touch our faces while asleep (hands and nails contain germs).
- Not to use heavy make-up to cover imperfections as it can further irritate sensitive skin and clog up the pores, preventing the skin from breathing and leading to infection. A special drying agent in a tinted cream, sold in tubes by most chemists, helps hide and reduce pimples to a certain extent.
- If acne fails to respond to a skin and pore wash, she should see her family doctor or a dermatologist. Another form of treatment is with tetracycline but this is only available on prescription.[2]
- To exercise at least three times a week for thirty minutes. Not only is this of benefit aerobically, but it also gives skin a healthy glow. Perspiring opens pores and helps release all that oil which causes those pimples that devastate the self-confidence of teenagers everywhere.

BREASTS AND THE ONSET OF MENSTRUATION

Puberty for girls may start as early as nine but can be as late as sixteen or seventeen. The average age for the start of periods is now twelve years and nine months. Girls who exercise strenuously, play lots of sport or are involved with ballet (and diet strictly) often start menstruating later. If your daughter hasn't menstruated by sixteen, take her to your family doctor.

The first signs of puberty are enlarged nipples and the growth of pubic hair. Pubic hair growth often starts as young as ten or eleven, and breasts start mounding slightly later.

Your daughter may be embarrassed by her developing breasts, if she is physically ahead of her friends. She may attempt to cover budding breasts by wearing baggy T-shirts or by slouching. Reassure her that her breasts are a sign of approaching womanhood and her future ability to nurture children. Encourage good posture and advise that she could be unhappy if she remained flat-chested all her life. Tell her that throughout history artists, poets and writers have celebrated the beauty of the female form and especially of female breasts. Many women have been so worried about being flat-chested they have foolishly risked their lives to have silicone implants.

Girls who mature later than their friends often fear something is wrong with them. They need understanding and reassurance from parents and good advice. Take your daughter to a specialist lingerie shop that employs a trained fitter so she can be taught how a good bra should fit, without the straps cutting into her shoulders. Juliet's breasts will continue to grow until she reaches sixteen or seventeen. Breasts may be rounded or conical and the shapes of nipples vary. Other changes at puberty are an increase in height and weight. Hips get bigger with a build-up of fatty tissue around the pelvic area — a natural preparation for bearing children.

As well as changes to her body, Juliet also has to cope with new and often disturbing sexual feelings. In addition there will be increased demands in her high school studies. No wonder tempers flare and she has confrontations with you and other siblings.

Your daughter may now start to withdraw from the family. This doesn't mean she is rejecting *you* — she's just growing up.

She needs time alone in her room to peer at herself in a mirror and reassess herself.

The following very simple explanation may be sufficient for your first mother-daughter talk on menstruation (the word comes from *mensis,* the Latin for month).

Explain that we use the word 'menstruation' to mean a regular monthly discharge from the uterus of blood vessels and tiny pieces of the lining of the uterus. A single human egg is released each month by one of two ovaries and travels down a tube to the uterus. If the egg is fertilised, it becomes embedded in the brownish cushioned lining of the uterus and a baby develops. If the egg remains unfertilised, the egg (along with the brown cushioned lining and those additional blood vessels) dissolves and emerges through the vaginal opening. Monthly periods vary in intensity and interval from 22-35 days. Most last around 5-6 days. The discharge is initially red in colour, then changes to brown.

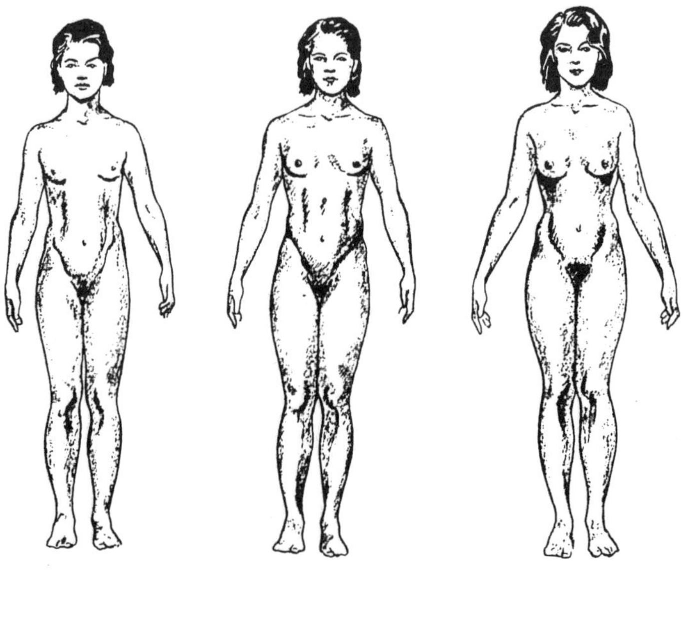

Early puberty Mid puberty Late puberty

HOW *you* CAN HELP

TALK ABOUT MENSTRUATION BEFORE IT HAPPENS

- Don't put it off. *After* her monthly periods arrive, your daughter may turn secretive and flatly *refuse* to talk about sex and reproduction. Find the right moment and have a quiet talk, *not* a lecture. Show her some sanitary pads and tampons and explain how they absorb menstrual discharge. Warn her to change her tampon at least every six hours initially and never use one if the outer wrapping has been broken or damaged as a precaution against toxic shock.
- Tell her, 'As you'll be getting monthly periods soon, it's important you know what to do. If you use a pad, it must be changed at *least* three times a day when bleeding is heavy. Some, but not all, authorities recommend using a sanitary pad rather than a tampon at night.'
- Your daughter's skin glands will change after puberty. It's vital she uses a good deodorant because the skin glands in her armpits and groin are perspiring more and could cause body odour, which will be unpleasant for others.
- Don't be gloomy and serious when discussing menstruation. In tribal societies women celebrate menstruation with dancing and singing, seeing it as breaking through the barrier between childhood and womanhood — not something unpleasant.
- If she is not at home when her first discharge starts, she should place a thick wad of toilet paper in her underwear. If it happens at school, she should go to the school nurse, who will give her a sanitary pad to wear. If she gets cramps she should lie down and take an aspirin; soaking in a warm bath helps some women.
- Reassure her that during her periods, she can swim, dance, run, exercise, wash her hair, swim, shower and, of course, take a bath.
- If your daughter's periods are very heavy or last more than six days, or she has 'spotting' in between, take her to a GP. Many girls prefer to see a woman doctor when it comes to discussing intimate matters.

PREMENSTRUAL STRESS

Adolescence for most girls is marked by exuberant energy and loads of activities at school. This 'awakening' to life's possibilities and the need to study can lead to overtiredness, with far too many activities crowded into a day. Lessons, sport, extracurricular activities and after-school commitments, as well as homework and part-time jobs, eat into time and energy. The result is that in the week prior to the onset of a period, you have a daughter who is overtired, stressed, easily upset and generally difficult — all ingredients for a family row.

Seasonal ills such as influenzas and colds can seriously set your daughter back if she is not eating properly and getting proper rest. Lack of concentration, irritability and tearfulness are all warning signals that some reassessment of priorities may be in order and that a day off school may also be appropriate.

SEXUALLY EXPLICIT MAGAZINES

Girls today are very aware of their developing bodies. Various teenage magazines, like *Dolly,* which have a no-holds-barred approach to the subjects they cover, target very young girls. They write freely about dating, sexual behaviour and orgasms. Some parents find the explicitness of today's teenage magazines worrying. Editors of these magazines are sales-driven, with the only restraint being a fear that adverse community response will scare off advertisers. Occasionally they take a more responsible approach and have a special issue dealing with sex and sexuality — in sealed supplements. On the positive side, they do warn teenagers about the dangers of HIV-AIDS, sexually transmitted infections and unwanted pregnancies, written in everyday language girls can understand. Some sealed supplements have given very sensible advice and stress one very important fact ignored by boys, that 'talking will bring you and a boy far closer together than sex ever will'.

As a marketing ploy sex information has proved very successful with teenagers, buying up these issues out of their pocket money. They experience the thrill of opening up a sealed section, usually dealing with topics which some Grade 10 girls had found 'boring' when they were discussed during 'Personal Health and Development Courses'!

According to one suburban newsagent, girls up to twelve buy *Girlfriend*, which the newsagent's seven-year-old daughter was allowed to read.[3] But what the little girl *really* wanted was a chance to read *Dolly*. However, her mother flatly refused to buy or give her a copy until she would be twelve. *Dolly* is read widely by girls as young as twelve and thirteen, but at fifteen most move on to *Cleo,* which is far *more* sexually explicit and aimed at an older market.

Your daughter is growing up in an era when sex is widely exploited for commercial purposes. She can see explicit sex scenes every day on TV, video and film. It is sensible to view adult TV programs with her and use the program as a basis for discussion of issues raised.

SEX, VAGINAL INFECTIONS AND CONTRACEPTION

Dr Jean Sparling says there is evidence that girls who receive the most information are those least likely to develop dangerous sexual habits. She stresses from personal experience in general practice that the emphasis on safety for girls has changed from the need to avoid pregnancy to the very real dangers of sexually transmitted infections and violence. Remember, AIDS and Hepatitis B can kill!

'Children will absorb knowledge about sex from points outside the home if *you* don't talk about it,' Dr Sparling says. She adds that the importance and limitations of condoms should be pointed out to the adolescent just before the onset of puberty, which may now be as young as eleven. It *must* be firmly instilled in your daughter that her body is to be respected by her and *everyone else* with whom she is in contact.

When you discuss sexual matters with your ten-year-old daughter, it is not necessary to discuss foreplay or oral sex, unless she specifically asks about them. But you should make sure that you discuss not only what happens to her body at puberty, but also other issues associated with sexual relationships. These include sexual feelings, sexual behaviour, contraception, pregnancy, sexually transmitted infections and protection from them.

This is the time when girls have sexual fantasies and pin posters of favourite pop or film idols to their bedroom walls. Many go much further. A survey by La Trobe University, Melbourne, reveals that by Year 12, 48% of schoolgirls have had sexual intercourse; a significant number would have started much younger.[4] If you are shocked, bear in mind that Shakespeare's Juliet was only thirteen when she first had sex with Romeo — as we all know, that relationship, like those of many immature couples, was doomed.

The first experience of sexual intercourse for young girls under seventeen is usually unplanned — it happens after a party

AIDS and Hepatitis B are lethal, so the safe sex message is paramount (The Australian Magazine, February, 1995)

and is often associated with alcohol consumption (some 6% admitted to having had 9-12 drinks before it happened). Under the circumstances it is not surprising that the survey revealed only a minority used condoms.

One positive fact to emerge from this survey was that 59% of girls in today's long-term relationships were using condoms. An interesting fact was the decrease in the number of sexual partners reported by sexually active students. In 1997 16% of sexually active students had three or more sexual partners, compared with 22% in 1992, with fewer using condoms early in the 1990s.

Myra Kostash's survey of Canadian teenage girls and other research in Europe, Australia and America has revealed that schoolgirls as young as thirteen and fourteen are emotionally blackmailed into sex by teenage boyfriends, well before they were ready for it.[5] Many admitted sadly they had encountered lust rather than love and did not really enjoy the sex act.

SO WHY *DO* SCHOOLGIRLS HAVE SEX ?

- **Young and immature girls often feel pressured into having sex: the boyfriend expects 'it' from them.**
- **The insecure girl lacks self-esteem and is very afraid of losing her boyfriend.**
- **Girls with disturbed home lives are acting out their problems and their desperate need for love and attention — any attention being better than none.**
- **The 'wild' adventurous girls want to try it.**
- **Group expectation (peer pressure) is that a sexual relationship is included in the definition of having a boyfriend.**
- **They are looking for romance but instead of the love they expected they experience only lust.**

Most girls are curious about sex, as they see it everywhere on television, film and video, but hope for long-term romantic involvement as well. They don't want to sleep around, because they fear that by doing so they could get a bad reputation and risk losing their girlfriends *and* the boyfriend. By Grade 10 most girls are beginning to experience oestrogen and other hormonal surges and sexual dreams. One 15-year-old girl in Grade 10 admitted she thought 'sexually active' meant kissing a boy behind the bike shed. Once the girl understood the meaning of the word, she volunteered that four girls in her class were on the pill and in relationships. One, like Nabokov's Lolita, disillusioned by the poor technique of boys, now had sex in return 'for presents' usually supplied by middle aged men.[6]

The Latrobe University survey revealed that many girls indicated they were disappointed by sex and the boy's lack of closeness or commitment to any ongoing relationship, other than a sexual one. Substantial numbers of girls on the pill fail to realise that it gives no protection against sexually transmitted infections. A misguided 18% were relying on withdrawal as a contraceptive and an anti-AIDS preventative; 9% were using the morning-after pill.[7]

Most sexually active schoolgirls were aware they could get pregnant from the very first time they had intercourse. They knew the dangers of contracting AIDS and that using condoms was sensible, but most admitted they hadn't insisted on using them. Some girls said they had unprotected sex because they had been 'too drunk' or 'high' on recreational drugs to put up resistance. Embarrassment, and not wanting to be accused of promiscuity, stopped girls from buying condoms or getting their doctor to prescribe the pill before having sex for the first time (or the second or the third). The use of contraceptives should be a joint responsibility, but many boys *still* believe that girls should take care of contraception.

TEENAGE GIRLS' ATTITUDES TO SEXUAL ACTIVITY:

- **A 'nice' girl can have sex, but only with one boy who 'loves' her and *cannot* change partners frequently.**
- **Girls monitor each other's conduct fiercely and can drop any girl from their group who is seen as a 'slut' or 'wild girl', even if the girl was pressured into having sex.**

FALLING IN LOVE

Be prepared for an emotional roller coaster if your teenager does fall in love. Teenage love is just as intense, romantic, idealistic and devastating as love in older couples. Nevertheless, many adults think schoolkids are too young to be truly in love.

In spite of the Sexual Revolution, the old double standard still survives. Fine for boys, but if a girl plays by the same rules she's stigmatised. If girls say no, in the eyes of many boys they're 'prick teasers', frigid or lesbian. Sometimes girls have sex to remain part of a sexually active clique of girls, or because they believe that male cliche, 'If you *really* loved me, you'd let me'. One reason why an inexperienced girl who makes love with a teenage boy fails to achieve an orgasm is because the boy is equally inexperienced.

Of course you will be protective of your daughter and wary of her boyfriend's intentions. For your daughter's sake respect their feelings for each other, don't be overly intrusive because you fear what might happen. If they intend to have sex, they will find an opportunity. Now it is vital your daughter is adequately informed about contraception and sexually transmitted infections. You might be happier if she were chaperoned all the time but that no longer happens. When first love coincides with final year exams and there is a conflict between spending time together and the need to study, parents must exercise forbearance together with firmness. Remind the lovesick couple of priorities and the need to look together to their futures.

CULTURAL DIFFERENCES

Among certain cultures it is not acceptable for a girl to go out unchaperoned with a boy, especially with someone from a different religious or cultural background. *Any* relationship not approved by the family can have serious consequences. Living in a foreign country, with customs that are contrary to strongly held religious beliefs, and fearing for their children lead some migrant parents to reject the idea of the daughter having close friendships outside the family circle. The girl's need to assimilate and cope with conflicting pressures can cause great distress to her and her parents — some girls become depressed as a result.

HOW *you* CAN HELP

WARN HER ABOUT THE PERILS OF SEX WITHOUT LOVE AND UNPROTECTED SEX

- Society has changed enormously. You may have been brought up to believe teenage sex is very wrong, but most girls no longer believe this and do not value chastity. Your responsibility is to warn your daughter of the risks of pregnancy or sexually-transmitted infections and explain the difference between love and lust. Her self-esteem should include her body. Sex without previously establishing a loving relationship with her partner short-changes her and will lower her self-esteem.
- Forewarn her about the old male trick of complaining of intolerable or lethal pain from an erection if she doesn't 'go all the way'. The standard female retort should be, 'If you *die*, you'll make medical history — no one else *ever* has.'
- Discuss the way pressure can be put on girls by boys using the line: 'If you *really* loved me, you would.' The answer to this one is, 'If you *really* loved me you wouldn't ask.'
- Should *she* decide to take a sexual partner, stress that **condoms must be worn every time** to minimise the risks of catching sexually-transmitted infections (see chapter on 'Dangerous Sex') as well as preventing pregnancy. Always check the use-by date of condoms to ensure they are effective.
- Doctors warn that it's possible to catch sexually-transmitted infections through oral as well as vaginal sex. To prevent risk from oral sex, special oral condoms (called Glydes) should be used.
- If she has a boyfriend and you think she may be trying to make up her mind whether to have vaginal sex, it may help to point out that mutual masturbation scarcely raises an eyebrow in today's world: **getting pregnant most certainly will**.

BULLYING AND STEALING

BULLYING OR BEING BULLIED

Roughly one child in every six undergoes some form of bullying.[1] Bullied children tend to be timid, nervous, small for their age and perceived by other kids as being 'different'. They may have a stutter or speech impediment, a 'funny' or foreign name, wear shabby or unfashionable clothes, or be bad at sport. Some bullied kids are really square pegs in round holes. A good example of this is academic girls who have been sent to sport-orientated schools, where other kids despise them for sucking up to the teacher, or being a swot. Bullies tend to blame their victims, offering feeble excuses for picking on victims like, 'It's all *their* fault. They look *odd*, wear *funny* clothes, speak *wrong*.'

Girl bullies can be just as bad as boys; their tactics can include hair pulling, scratching of faces and destruction of schoolbooks. The victim may be locked inside a room, have uniform, school bags or possessions stolen or damaged, receive unsigned 'hate mail' or rude drawings.

A great deal of bullying by girls is psychological. The victim, who feels unable to defend herself, is rejected, jeered at, taunted and teased. Another form of victimisation is being 'sent to Coventry', which means that no one in the class will speak to the unfortunate girl. Public rejection by a popular group or clique, which the victim openly or secretly longs to join, can damage self-image and confidence. Such pre-teen and teenage cliques foster hot-house friendships with warm embraces and shared confidences. Girls have an intense need for sharing experience with a 'best friend', although such intense relationships often shift and break down over time and new 'best friends' are sought.

The bullied girl can find herself rejected by class members for reasons which seem trivial to adults: having buck-teeth or a dental brace, acne, fuzzy hair, lacking the right clothes or sports equipment, or for wearing the wrong brand names. The victims may be tripped up or made to stand at the back of the line, ridiculed or called unpleasant names. Parents are frequently at a loss when their child pleads with them not to make things worse by telling the school authorities. The victim fears that there will be reprisals if they 'tell' — although this *is* the best course of action, as bullies thrive on threats and fears. Older children who bully often demand money, forcing their victims into stealing to 'pay off' their assailants. Victims lose marks at school when bullies destroy or damage homework, especially projects that have taken many hours to complete. Often several children, under an aggressive ringleader, pick on one child, making the bullied child's life a nightmare.

Most schools have changed their approach to bullying, which was once thought to be part and parcel of school life. Today, in these schools, complaints by parents are treated confidentially. One member of staff — a senior teacher, the deputy head, a school counsellor or a year coordinator — is nominated as the person to deal with bullying, rather than leaving it up to the victim's class teacher, who may well be young and relatively inexperienced in dealing with the problem.

In many schools the incidence of bullying is being lowered by parents and teachers working together to isolate and punish bullies. At class meetings bullies can be named. In some schools bullies are 'outed' in front of their class to release their hold over others, made aware of the effects of their behaviour and isolated at playtime. Recommendations can be made for counselling, for psychological treatment or in severe cases the bully can be expelled. 'Buddy' schemes, where an older child is appointed as a younger child's mentor, have worked very well in reducing or even stopping the incidence of bullying.

DETRIMENTAL EFFECTS OF BULLYING

Bullied children often complain about feeling sick or having abdominal pains before going to school. They can have nightmares, eating disorders, and bed-wetting may become a problem. Victims can become so depressed that some have contemplated suicide as a way out — a small number, suffering problems at home as well as at school, have even succeeded.[2]

Some victims have overdosed with pills (the classic cry for help) but have been rescued in time.

Danger signals by 'depressed' adolescents, contemplating suicide, range from talking about death and giving away prized possessions to failing even their best subjects at school.

Being bullied can have long-lasting effects on the victims' health — both physical and mental. Children constantly teased or 'isolated' by classmates in their early and pre-teen years show poorer mental and physical health during the final years of school.

Overweight girls, teased and given names like 'Fatty' or 'Thunder Thighs', often start crash diets or fasts that lead to their becoming anorexic or bulimic. Children with names that sound 'funny' (and children include foreign names in this category) are often teased unmercifully. Be very careful when choosing your daughter's first name. Parents should be aware that the 'cute' name they chose for their baby girl may sound stupid when yelled out around the playground. A girl called Willow Legge was teased unmercifully because she was a dumpy, obese schoolgirl — Willow's mother, Mrs Wanda Legge, a former model, had expected her daughter to become a tall, willowy beauty.

Parents, together with the child's class teacher, should try to build up the victim's self-esteem and help her to become more assertive. In some cases it has helped if the victim is taught to 'walk tall', answer back clearly and, if her voice is high and squeaky, to deepen it.

The victim should pretend not to care but answer threats of violence by assuring the bully that, if it continues, she will tell her parents, who will report her (or him) to the school principal.

A Real-life Story

HOW TO BEAT BULLIES

Klaus Strumpf came to Australia to set up retail outlets for his company in Germany. He, his wife Christina and his young daughter Angelika settled in Brisbane, which had a reputation for being a friendly place. Although the whole family had taken intensive English classes before coming to Australia, Angelika had trouble in understanding the Aussie accent. Her classmates at the local primary school laughed at her 'funny' foreign accent and what seemed to them her equally 'funny' name.

As Angelika loved learning, she wanted to do well in class and was desperately keen to 'fit in'. But she found herself isolated in a school where sport was idolised. She no longer received good marks and she began to dread going to school. All the other girls had friends or were part of some group, but Angelika had no one. She was never invited to other children's homes or parties. She became withdrawn and miserable, but said nothing at home, as she didn't want her mother to 'make a fuss', fearing that it would worsen the situation.

Just before her last term, Angelika came home with her schoolbag damaged and her text books torn. She revealed her classmates had teased her unmercifully. They had laughed at her because she could not swim and was afraid of water. Angelika burst into tears and said that she wanted to go back to Germany.

Recognising that Angelika had a problem, Christina arranged private swimming lessons and, slowly, her daughter overcame her psychological fear of water. Once she had learned to swim she became more self-confident.

Before Angelika started secondary school she met Melanie through the Lutheran Church. Having just moved to Brisbane from Melbourne, Melanie was also apprehensive about being 'a new girl'. Christina invited Melanie round to her house for tea, so Angelika had a friend before they both started secondary school. The two girls got on well together. They were both interested in music and singing.

At secondary school, Angelika found herself allotted to the care of an older girl in a higher class as part of the 'buddy' system. This time she fitted in well as it was a far more academic school.

Now, two years later, Angelika speaks fluent English and is always near the top of her class. Her talents for music and singing have been recognised and she is enjoying her new life in Australia. Angelika and Melanie remain 'best friends' and have both been picked to tour with the school choir.

HOW *you* CAN HELP

- If you suspect your daughter is being bullied, but she denies it, watch for torn exercise books, bruises or scratches, damage to clothes or other personal belongings. Danger signs can be loss of appetite, stammering, nervous tics, bed-wetting, nail-biting, sleepwalking, sleep-talking or frequent loss of lunch money or her packed lunch. She may come home hungry and conceal the fact.
- Once you are convinced she is being bullied, reassure her that it is in no way *her* fault. This is vital to raise her self-esteem. Remind her she is a terrific kid and praise her often. Make her more assertive by role-playing. You should assume the role of a bully and coach her how to respond appropriately.
- Contact the deputy head or the class teacher to find out which staff member is responsible for dealing with bullying. Don't get upset. Request information as to whether other pupils are being bullied by the same child. If necessary present any evidence, such as photographs of injuries or damaged property. The school will investigate and deal with the matter, which is now acknowledged as a serious problem in schools. In severe and persistent cases bullies will be isolated from their classes, sent for counselling or could, in severe cases, be expelled.
- Encourage your daughter to get involved with a sport, with music or any other activity she enjoys, so that she is viewed by her classmates as being 'good' at some activity.
- Socialising is an essential part of the learning process. Talk to other mothers in your daughter's class. It is important your daughter has friends. Invite a few girls from her class for a birthday party: kids who have birthday parties tend to be invited to the birthdays of others.
- If your daughter's problems are not being addressed, clearly she is not at the right school for *her*. She might benefit from being moved to a smaller, independent school. Montessori or Rudolf Steiner schools have helped in some cases.

PEER GROUPS AND CLIQUES

Groups or cliques, so dear to most girls, start in primary school and continue through secondary school. It seems that most girls' groups are more concerned with keeping others out and sharing 'secrets' than achieving any particular aim.

Younger girls still at primary school are usually not yet interested in boys. At that stage, they are likely to view boys as stupid and giggle about them. On the other hand, secondary school cliques are full of girls who spend a great deal of time talking about boyfriends, clothes and going out together. Some of those girls, who are already sexually involved with boys, discuss their emotions and experiences with their peers or best friends.

During her teenage years, when your daughter is asserting her own identity and moves away from you, she could well feel that belonging to a peer group is very important. Not being part of a group or clique, or not having a 'best friend', could lower her self-esteem. Friendships at that age are quite fluid and she will eventually find a 'soul mate' outside of school, if not *at* school.

SHOPLIFTING MEANS STEALING

Some girls steal because they are troubled, others do it for kicks. Like adult shoplifters, children often steal what they perceive could (in a distorted way) replace a vital element missing from their hearts and their lives. Others steal to keep up with their group or clique (the 'Buy-A-Friend' syndrome). Some girls steal because they are bullied into it: a few, like some adults, feel they have the right to take what they want. Stealing from shops or homes by teenagers can indicate a drug habit. Many small children attempt to steal something from the lower shelves at supermarkets. By the time they turn seven they should know that stealing is *not* like borrowing and will cause big trouble if they are caught.

HOW *YOU* CAN HELP

- You should have pointed out from early childhood to your daughter the difference between what is *mine, yours* and *theirs*. Make her apologise to shopkeepers or classmates and take back in person *anything* she has stolen. Insist she gives something *extra* back or does something as a compensation to anyone she has wronged.
- Leaving money in a jar in the kitchen acts as a deterrent (and takes the thrill out of stealing). Your daughter and her siblings have to write an IOU with their name on it when taking money out of the jar *and* pay it back out of their own pocket money.
- Open a savings account for your daughter, however small. Encourage her to save a proportion of her pocket money or earnings from a part-time job. Ask her how *she* would feel if the bank stole money from *her*.
- If stealing continues, involve school counsellors or (informally) ask the police for advice. Many police forces now have juvenile counsellors to deal with such situations. No one wants their children to grow up with a police record, least of all the police. **Remember, courts now make parents pay for their children's theft or vandalism**. If one is available, try to join a parents' support group for counselling and support over the problem.

BODY PIERCING AND TATTOOS

Journalist Kate Collins has done some research into why teenage girls spend good money (often earned from part-time jobs) having their bodies tattooed and metal objects attached to their anatomy. Although body piercing may distress you as a parent, do not panic if your daughter announces one day she is off to the piercing shop. Kate can see the funny side of what is, for most girls, only a passing fashion.

Once upon a time 'nice gels' got their ears pierced as a rite of passage. They chose a pair of simple pearls or gold hoops, nothing Jane Austen wouldn't approve of. Only Tibetans and Hindus wore rings in their noses, only Black Uhlans and sailors wore tattoos.

Tattooing — or tats as they are now universally known — became a high-fashion item around the same time as body piercing. Both are a subcultural language, instantly readable to initiates. If you don't know what a guiche is, or a Prince Albert, or what wearing an earring in the left ear for males means, go to a body piercing shop or a tattooist and ask. You'll get a guarded or downright hostile reception — they'll assume you're from the State Health Department (who receive a wide range of complaints from worried parents) or a newspaper reporter — but be polite, non-threatening and persevere.

What started this sudden lemming-like urge among teens to turn their bodies into dartboards and colanders? One could blame it on their parents, the Sixties generation, for trekking off on the Hippy Trail and dragging home ideas gained in the Third World. You could also blame Demi Moore and Madonna for getting bored with wearing their bras on the outside and turning to torso tats and henna hands as a novelty. Above all, *don't* panic if it happens, stay calm and look for a silver (or gold) lining. Try seeing tats and piercing as degrees in a learning curve and the passing fads and fancies of teenagers.

Tats last longer than henna hands, which are relatively cheap to have painted on but wear off after a few weeks. There are henna transfers for the wrists, which are inexpensive and sold by some chemists. They resemble delicate henna artwork, peel off a roll, stick to wrists, then fade away.

Tattoos take a long time to apply (and remove by laser). The *big* risk in both tattooing and piercing is infection: dirty or re-used needles, cross infection, hepatitis or worse. If your daughter announces she plans to get a tattoo, don't shout or get annoyed. Sit down with her and ask some relevant questions which will, hopefully, make your daughter think twice — 'Are you doing this to please your boyfriend or to demonstrate just how unique or independent you are?'

Tell her that tattoos are expensive to remove (around $1,000 to remove a small one by laser surgery, a cost not covered by health insurance). She should think of the future and the cost of removal. On a schoolgirl or university student a curling vine or a blue and red dragon twisting its way round wrist and arm may seem cute today, but could be embarrassing in the future. Does she plan to work in a conservative occupation, where she could be forced to hide her tattoo with long sleeves, however hot the weather? If, instead of the dragon, she has her current boyfriend's name and a heart tattooed high on the inside of her thigh, could so intimate a tattoo cause problems if entering into a new relationship?

Piercing is far less drastic than tattooing, but easier to remove. The main types of piercing are: nose (septum or nostril, which require different techniques), tongue (high infection risk), navel, eyebrow, bridge (between eyes). Genital piercing is surprisingly popular — clitoris or labia for girls, scrotum (guiche) or penis (the dreaded Prince Albert) for boys.

Reputable Health Department-approved shops (not that Health Departments do approve of many of them) should use autoclaves and single-use disposable needles. Make sure the person piercing your daughter's body is aware of the risks of transmitting Hepatitis B by using contaminated needles. Nipple and navel rings should not be too thin or they can catch on clothes and tear away, causing pain and infection. Use only proper Department of Health-inspected practitioners, no talented friends doing a cheap piercing job in their garages. Legally, your daughter can't get pierced or tattooed without your approval until she's seventeen. Piercing and/or tattooist shops should have a sign on the wall warning about health risks, such as hepatitis and sepsis, and the legal requirement that for *anyone* under the age of 17 parental approval is required by law. Really? Tell that to the growing number of pubescent girls who, despite being barely tall enough to see over the counter, seem to have no trouble at all getting nose, navel, nipple, tongue, eyebrow, bridge, ear or — ouch! yes, even *there* — studded with silver, titanium or stainless steel rings, bolts and stars.

Adolescents are the *last* people to take notice of warnings about legal age limits for anything — from sex to drinking to sticking things into themselves. That's why pubs and clubs demand ID. Passing yourself off as older than you really are is a teenage art form perfected by years of getting into M-rated movies; it's a group conspiracy in which unscrupulous piercing or tats practitioners are only too happy to collude for hard cash.

One well-known piercing business came perilously close to being sued recently when it inserted a navel ring into a fifteen-year-old; her father, a prominent lawyer, nearly sued when his daughter's piercing became infected. No wonder many practitioners are shy when it comes to talking about the pitfalls. Not that they've got much time to talk. In most piercing shops today, queues of eager girls wait their turn to be punctured, standing in line beside display cases of metal rings and beaded accessories.

Legal warnings are strictly window-dressing. It's *highly* unlikely that your average fifteen-year-old gives them a second glance, particularly if she's already had a row with an anguished parent, who has strictly forbidden her to have a navel/nipple/nasal/-tongue/eyebrow insertion. Those busy people behind the counter will *not* fix your offspring with a steely glare and demand proof of her age before they pierce her under-age body. Get real. This is the 1990s, the Era of Individual Responsibility, right?

Try to take comfort from the fact that what we're talking about here is much bigger than your daughter turning her navel into a flip-top beer can or her earlobe into something that would look right under the bonnet of a sports car. This isn't torture, this is fashion. The bad 'F' word. Peer pressure, cutting-edge hype. An industry with its own teen idol gods and goddesses and media gurus handing down commandments from on high. The Viper Club in Hollywood and the pages of *Dolly* magazine, that Bible of bimbo-hood, make the rules. Parents trying to compete with what Gwyneth or Keanu or Smashing Pumpkins dictate should realise they haven't a hope of succeeding.

Before you start blaming it all on premature weaning, or your decision to put your kid into care and go back to work, let's take a look at some sobering figures.

Q. Which is the biggest single consumer market in the post-Spice world?

A. Thirteen-to-nineteen-year-old girls, of course. In Australia alone, there are nearly 900,000 of them, many with over $66 a week to spend.

Q. What do they spend it on?

A. Consumer goods and entertainment.

In the USA, female teenage spending surged 4% in the last two years. This is serious consumerism, the kind that makes the cosmetic, fashion, fast food, music and movie industries behave like

Dracula in a blood bank. In 1996-97, Australian teenagers (many with part-time jobs while still at school) spent $88.6 million per week, $4.6 billion a year — an 18% rise on 1995. And it's still climbing.

Q. And which is the biggest single entity within this group?

A. Girls, aged 16-17, according to *Dolly* magazine's 1997 Youth Report. And guess what? The girls who are being pierced are getting younger every year.

Q. What is the new market?

A. Sub-teens. *Sub* as in ten-year-old girls. That's right. This group, frightening in its social power, may spend only an average of $14 per capita a week, weaseled out of their pocket-money-paying parents. But self-obsessed, peer-driven and with a pack mentality rivalled only by Canadian timber wolves, by God, they'll spend it on drawing attention to themselves and, by so doing, looking as much like each other as possible. Some people reckon tattoos and body piercing show that teenagers are deeply insecure and just want to follow the latest fad. Surveys showed that while only 23% of teenage boys wanted to be better looking, 40% of girls did. Bad self-image, as the behavioural gurus put it.

So that's why Juliet is hobbling round on her 30-centimetre orthopaedic platforms that make even Chinese bound feet look sensible. That's why she did that strange thing, involving green dye with purple stripes to her gelled hair. That's why she has black nails and bits of metal sticking out of every orifice. It's not that she's trying to get at you. She's just the same entity that you were back in the Sixties, a dedicated follower of fashion.

The answer to all parents' worries is that what goes in your daughter's body, may, eventually come out or off. By the time your sixteen-year-old turns eighteen, sanity and a more clearly developed sense of aesthetics will, hopefully, prevail. If not, chances are the inserted objects will get infected and have to come out very soon on health grounds. This happened to Kate's child. The obvious discomfort was a joy to watch, a learning curve in stoicism as much as a practical lesson in the dangers of being a fashion victim.

Responsible practitioners will emphasise that the wounds (which is what tats and piercings are) must be kept scrupulously clean with antiseptic lotion and customers *must* return for checkups afterwards. How soon or how often depends on the procedure. If the piercing shows signs of infecting, the ring/stud/*whatever* should be immediately removed and the hole allowed to heal over. Voila! — the piercee has far too many painful memories to go through the whole procedure again.

Infection is a long-term hazard, especially if autoclaves have not been used to sterilise instruments. Even the information leaflets handed out to would-be piercees by professional piercers admit as much. Tell-tale signs of infection she (and you) should look for are:-

- **seepage of pus around the metal**
- **rashes or blotchy red marks around the piercing.**

Sounds inviting, doesn't it? It's even more unlikely that the about-to-be-pierced teenager bothers to read the fine-print warnings. If she did, she'd worry that piercings are done without anaesthetic.

Doctors and dentists are specific about the inherent dangers of infections. The Australian Dental Association particularly dislikes tongue or lip piercing, because of the higher risk of infection associated with the mouth. Food and plaque are likely to cause major problems when it comes to keeping any new wound clean in the mouth. Even if the piercing heals cleanly, infection can occur years later, and with tongue or lip rings or studs chipped or eroded tooth enamel is a definite problem. So is the danger of choking, should a tongue ring or stud backing come loose and be swallowed, *particularly* while the wearer is asleep.

Navels are also dangerous places to put foreign objects, from the point of view of hygiene. As the Bible's Song of Solomon points out, a bowl-shaped navel can be a charming receptacle for holding fluids. Unfortunately, with a piece of metal stuck through your daughter's navel, that fluid is far more likely to be pus from a weeping wound than your Biblical honey or wine. Wine? The only whine you're likely to hear from *your* teenage navel ring wearer is 'Oooh, Mum, it *hurts*!'

The techniques used to pierce your daughter vary for different parts of the anatomy. Experts discourage home piercing kits and insist piercing equipment should be sterilised in an autoclave. An earring can be inserted using a kind of staple-gun. This isn't feasible for the nose, which has much harder cartilage in the septum and nostrils than the ear. A nose ring requires the use of a special piercing needle, which should come fresh out of its wrapper. So does the nipple pierce. As for the clitoral pierce, anyone prepared to undergo this without anaesthetic is likely to be beyond reasoning.

When your daughter announces she is about to get pierced, do *not* scream at her. Instead, just as you did when she wanted a dragon tattooed on her arm, ask calmly:

- **How *do* you feel about having a large piercing needle or stud gun stuck into you *without* an anaesthetic?**
- **How *will* you pay your dental bills when your teeth start looking as though you've been chewing beer cans?**
- **How *do* you plan to stop choking to death during the night if/when the metal stud through your tongue falls out?**
- **How *do* you go through the airport metal detector without setting alarms ringing, leading to a full body search?**

If sweet reasoning fails, accept the inevitable with grace. Be sympathetic, but keep a close eye on her health: insist she continues bathing the pierced area with antiseptic. Hang in there, Mum! Remember, *all* teenage fads have their day, then go out of fashion.

NAVEL RINGS AND DAUGHTERS

All hell broke loose during dinner when pretty, dark-haired Sally, two months short of her sixteenth birthday, announced that she had her navel pierced and a ring inserted. Her parents stared in disbelief as she pulled up her T-shirt to confirm what they hoped was a bad joke.

Sally was considerate, affectionate, seemingly unaffected by teenage angst, extraterrestrial hair, black nail polish, etc. Her parents' first response was reproach. How *could* she have done something so dangerous, so foolish, so horrible? What right did she have to mutilate her body? It must be removed... immediately! All normal reactions!

Sally remained cool, pointed to her mother's pierced ears and reminded her they had agreed three years ago she could have her ears pierced. Sally asserted her right to make decisions about her own body, replying to her parents' question as to the reason she had done this, that she liked the look. Full stop!

She assured her parents that she had gone to a reputable place which pierced hundreds of people. Under pressure she told the address and confirmed her parents' worst fears: a downtown arcade infamous for drop-outs, computer games and pinball machines.

The parents tried the medical danger approach. Was she aware of the dangers associated with these activities: hepatitis, tetanus, HIV infection from needles, dreadful scarring? Sally replied that she bathed the navel every few hours and was following instructions to keep it clean, as she had done when her ears were pierced.

They tried the bullying approach. She *had* to remove the ring. Point blank refusal. They pointed out that technically she was under the age to give consent and that under law the piercing establishment was guilty of assault, as she was a minor. Her parents informed her they were going to report the matter to the police, speak to the shop owner and their solicitor. Voices were raised. Sally began to cry. The parents thought they were getting somewhere. Then Sally announced that when she turned sixteen, she would leave home and *they* couldn't stop her.

Things were going from bad to worse. The parents didn't want Sally to leave home. They wanted her to remain at home but without that ring. And here she was saying that she *could* leave.

Her father said that there didn't appear to be any infection and that was their prime concern. He suggested the 'implant' be medically checked and advice sought about potential dangers should Sally contemplate further body decorating.

♥ A Real-life Story ♥

A Real-life Story

Mother didn't think this at all funny. Sally agreed to have the family doctor check her out and, if there were a problem, to remove the ring. Mother rang the surgery for an appointment and told the doctor that they wanted the ring removed and Sally given a strong talking to. The doctor examined Sally and explained some of the complications which could arise.

Mother looked grim and insisted he remove the ring here and now. The doctor looked from mother to daughter and asked whether Sally would agree to his removing the ring. This halted mother in her tracks. She had not considered the possibility that removal had to be consented to by her child. Mother insisted that her daughter agree. Sally burst into tears. The doctor, sympathetic to her distress, offered Sally a box of tissues and invited her into an adjoining room where she could compose herself.

While Sally was outside mother and doctor had a quiet talk. He reassured mother that there was no risk of infection and that the wound was healing well. He also pointed out he was not prepared to remove the ring *without* Sally's consent, as that would constitute assault. He advised the parents to try living with the navel ring until Sally, in all likelihood, removed it *herself* when she had outgrown this phase.

The parents spoke to the piercing shop's manager about the circumstances whereby a minor had not been asked for identification prior to the operation. The manager insisted that anyone who came in was asked for an ID. She was advised that a complaint had been made to the police (who had referred the matter to the Juvenile Aid Bureau) and that assault charges could be pending. The manager was frank about the problem of minors in her shop and said she could not afford to take the risk of piercing them or she could be sued and closed down. Her problem was that teenage girls' appearances were deceptive: they used ID cards of older friends, or even those of their friends' older sisters to establish 'proof' of their age.

The Juvenile Aid Bureau went to the piercing shop and spoke to the proprietors, warning them of the legal risk of not properly verifying identity and proof of age. After talking it over the parents agreed to take no further action. Sally did not flaunt her victory. Every time they caught a glimpse of the navel ring, her parents bit their tongue. In fact, a tongue ring would have been worse.

It seemed a long six months. Then, one day, Sally's navel ring was no longer there.

FLIGHT FROM THE NEST

LEAVING WITHOUT YOUR PERMISSION

Many young girls will run away from home, or discuss leaving home with their friends, in response to what they perceive as stressful relationships. Some, like the girl in our real-life story below, leave because they are sexually involved with a boy of their age. Sometimes they leave home for reasons that do not seem rational to parents. Therefore it is vital that you listen to what your daughter regards as problems with home and parenting. Try and have a discussion with her at a time that *you* choose, rather than one she chooses. Be well-prepared and stay calm, as teenagers can become totally irrational about measures you see as protecting them.

Beware those guilt traps into which many girls try to lead parents. You have provided a safe home, food and education, the Big Three of parenting. Point out to her quite clearly all the things you have done and which you believe are important for parenting, starting off with the fact that you are the person who loves her most. If she still decides to leave home without your permission, she will remember this when the going gets tough.

Before the age of sixteen, most girls have no idea of the dangers attached to leaving home and 'roughing it'. They honestly think they can manage alone, leaving parents frantic with worry.

In Australia the school leaving age is only fifteen although it is sixteen in most other developed countries. Strangely enough, from the parent's point of view, there are no hard and fast legal rulings about the age that children can leave home, although under common law (a body of knowledge built up over centuries), judges, when settling disputes, usually indicate children can leave home at sixteen. Be aware that *no* government department or its paid social workers can give your daughter permission to leave home; neither can they force children to return home.

Being a parent bestows few legal rights: we hear more today about the rights of the child, which are vital in Third World countries where children are paid a pittance to work long days or sold into sex slavery. However, children's rights can bring big problems when aired as gospel by wild teenagers in developed countries. At school girls repeat myths to each other about generous living-away-from-home allowances paid to runaway teenagers by the government. These myths arise because the allowances that are granted to some (but not all) children living away from home seem enormous to a girl who has never handled much money. Some girls, faced with a curfew for a late party or something similar, threaten parents through their sobs, 'Unless you let me go to So-and-So's party, I'll leave home, tell the social workers you abused me, get an allowance from the government and you'll *never* see me again!'

Wrong, of course. In earlier decades when many social reforms were initiated, it was far easier for kids to get a living-away-from-home allowance with fabrications about parental abuse, and some did so. Teenagers today, telling tales of parental abuse in order to obtain money, find themselves interviewed by well-trained social workers who will, in most cases, check out their stories rigorously.

Children often test their parents. Faced with threats of your daughter leaving home, calmly point out that she will find it very difficult now to justify applying for government living-away assistance. She will also find it hard to get temporary or part-time work. Do some sums with her. Show her just how much it costs to live in even the most basic type of rented accommodation. Unlike home, the phone she uses so much will no longer be free; laundry, food and transport will also cost money. Living on the streets is not the answer, as children are routinely hassled there for sex, beaten up or even murdered. Ask her why, if living away from home is so marvellous, these days it has become common for people in their twenties and thirties to return home and live with their parents.

DO TODAY'S KIDS BEHAVE WORSE THAN THEIR PARENTS DID?

A Real-life Story

Back in the 1970s, towards the end of the long summer holidays, my daughter Carla, then 14 years old, wanted to join her elder brother and his friend John (at that stage I didn't realise that she had a crush on John) to go grape picking in Mildura. Mum had already agreed. 'So it's all right with you too, Dad?' she asked.

I told Carla in no uncertain terms it was *not* all right with me. I reminded her that she had to go back to school within a month. Carla promised with her hand on her heart that she would be back before start of school. It took a great deal of persuading on her part, but eventually I acceded to her wish, as long as she kept her promise. 'Course I will!' promised Carla convincingly.

But when the holidays were over, Carla did *not* turn up. I felt hurt, angry and let down by my attractive but totally unreliable daughter. Fortunately, I knew from my son where all three of them were staying. My first impulse was to fly to Mildura (a long way from Brisbane!), find Carla and drag her home. I agonised all night and then considered it better to send her a plane ticket, accompanied by an urgent request that she return home forthwith.

Four days later a letter arrived from Carla with the plane ticket. 'Sorry, Dad, I'm staying with Hugh and John in Mildura.'

In despair I consulted the local police to find out what I could do as Carla was required by law to return to school until she was fifteen. The police officer shrugged, 'Why bother? This sort of thing happens all the time. She'll be back...eventually.' I gave up.

Carla returned home after she had her fifteenth birthday and was legally no longer required to go back to school — something she had no intention of doing anyhow.

The years passed. Carla, now thirty-six, is happily married and has three children. Justine, her eldest daughter, is receiving top marks at school and enjoys reading and learning tremendously.

Recently I reminded Carla of how she ran away from home when she was Justine's age. I asked her how she would respond if Justine should behave as she had done. An expression of horror appeared on her face 'Never, never would I allow Justine to do a thing like that!'

The irony is that Justine is determined to go to university and become a teacher and has no wish to take off from school. It proves that today's kids are not necessarily any worse than their parents and there is hope for their future.

MOVING OUT WITH YOUR BLESSING (WELL...SORT OF)

Your daughter is moving out and she is only seventeen, or eighteen. How well will she cope without you?

This is the ultimate test of your parenting skills and how you have prepared her for independence. Her reason for leaving could be to study or work in another town, to marry or to move in with friends or someone special. For the small town or country child, this transition from living in a close family, a small community where she is well known and knows everyone else, is a major milestone. Moving to another town or to a big city, establishing a new network of friends, adjusting to life in a college residence or a shared house can be a daunting experience.

Most girls cope well, in fact better than most boys, who seem to abandon the idea of laundry, clean sheets and socks when leaving home. There is all the excitement of new freedoms, meeting and getting along with a variety of people, managing limited finances, making choices about food, balancing work, leisure and sleep, coping with laundry and cleaning (as pointed out previously, many girls manage this very well). Your daughter will need to draw on inner strength to cope with loneliness, occasional sickness, decision making about jobs or courses which don't work out, and emotional ups and downs. These are survival skills that she has to learn.

Don't worry if Juliet is not good at keeping in touch with you and prefers to go off with friends on free weekends rather than come home. This means *you* have done well: she has adjusted to her new life.

YOUR DAUGHTER MOVES IN WITH HER LOVER

It is very hard for parents to accept that their daughter has moved in with a boyfriend, especially if there seems to be no apparent intention of marrying or making a lifelong commitment.

Parents are still very protective of daughters. Fathers feel their daughters are special and want to protect them from predatory males. They fear their daughter will be misused or her heart broken. Cultural backgrounds can make this situation particularly difficult to cope with. A family's religious beliefs and traditions about the role of men and women can make it difficult to accept the freedom of choice that women have gained for themselves in our society and the subsequent loss of authority of fathers or father figures.

Mother's relationship with her daughter can either be very close or confrontational. There is the temptation to see her decision to leave home as yet another example of wilfulness and perverseness. If mother and daughter are close, it can be very hard to bear the shift of emotional focus away from the family, especially if you do *not* approve of the boy or man involved. The heart tends to dominate in these decisions: it is risky to force your daughter to choose between him and you. You have to make yours as to whether she and her partner are welcome. If you accept the situation with grace, you will make it easier for her to return home should things not work out. If you reject her and decide not to condone what you consider to be 'an immoral or unwise situation', think carefully if you would judge a son's action as harshly. Remember Christmas is a good time for reunion.

YOUR DAUGHTER *WON'T* MOVE OUT

Some parents would like their adult children to experience life, be independent, get part-time work if they are students or, if already in the work force, leave home and start being responsible for their own lives. The parents themselves want to get on with their own interests, travel, see more of friends, move into a smaller house or flat requiring less work. But what happens? Their fledglings simply won't fly away.

Some cities are prohibitively expensive to live in and, unfortunately for this generation, moving out of home into rented or purchased accommodation is not nearly as easy as it was for their parents. It seems that anything they can afford is a 'dump' that gives parents nightmares.

Even so, whilst home is comfortable and convenient, there does come a time when young adults have to start earning their way, move out and take responsibility for their own lives. If your daughter is a student, she should be looking for part-time work. It *is* available, even with high unemployment, but may require more intensive effort and persistence to find it. If unemployed, she may be eligible for assistance and should be looking to improve her qualifications.

Encourage your daughter to move away from home by helping during the initial period with household items you don't need and a few groceries. Encourage her to visit regularly for meals and/or weekends. It is a good learning experience for her to have to budget for items like rent, electricity, phone bills, transport, food, clothing, etc.

YOUR DAUGHTER'S BOYFRIEND STAYS OVERNIGHT

Once upon a time, a young woman who met Mr Right became engaged and married, after which she moved from the parental home to live with her husband. In the 1970s, a young woman who met Mr Right moved in with him. Often her parents pretended not to know, 'keeping face' in front of friends and relatives. Marriage often followed after a trial period or when they decided to have children.

Today, a young woman sees premarital sex as normal. She meets Mr Right and introduces him to her parents, who invite him to stay for dinner. He stays the night. Her parents pretend not to notice when they both emerge from the daughter's bedroom the following morning. On subsequent visits this is repeated, with the young man often staying over the weekend.

Concerned for your daughter's well-being, you wonder about the young man's intentions. Should you assume there is a private understanding between them — something that was once known as a 'secret' or 'private' engagement?

Now that you have met the boyfriend, you may wish to find out something about his background. You should be clear whether you are prepared to accept a sexual relationship between your daughter and him under *your* roof. Are you going to treat him as a member of the family? Will you invite his parents over for dinner? Will they become part of your extended family?

FULL NEST PLUS BOYFRIEND

Gradually, your daughter and her boyfriend may spend more time at your home. If they are students or unemployed, the prospect of marriage would be very remote.

To all intents and purposes, they would be in a de facto relationship, while living in *your* home. If you are faced with this prospect, think hard. It's *your* home and it is up to you to decide whether you want to share it with your daughter's lover.

Parents facing this situation are confronted with unsatisfactory choices. Your values, cultural background and outlook will all have a bearing on your decisions. If you have a religious and cultural background which imposes traditional behaviour on women, your daughter's conduct and flouting of parental authority will be painful to you. Remember that women have equal rights and, by living in a Western environment, your daughter has been exposed to different cultural influences and acts accordingly.

If you are happy for your daughter's boyfriend to move in, make sure you set ground rules for joint living and *review* these rules every three or six months:

- **You must be able to maintain your privacy.**
- **Your daughter and her friend must not depend on you for money. They should have a joint income and contribute their fair share of food and other expenses.**
- **They *must* do their share of housework.**

One positive side of sharing is that you don't come home to an empty house, your daughter and her friend provide company and you may appreciate having them around. You are also providing a safe environment for young adults. These days it is far less common

than in the past for relatives — grandparents, aunts, uncles or older cousins — to provide a safe alternative to home.

If the couple are both working, the chances are they will eventually move out of your home and live together. However, as impecunious students, they will be dependent on parents and unable to afford to move out. In addition, as soon as they enter the work force in countries like Australia or America, where tertiary education is not free, they may have to pay off university fees — and all this at a time when previous generations of graduates got married, saved for a deposit on a house or bought a car. Small wonder that today far fewer middle-class twenty-somethings are thinking about marriage, buying homes and having kids.

Today, the decision to leave home is more often made by the young adult than ordered by parents. However, 'letting go' with grace and confidence is proof of good parenting and a way to ensure you *all* maintain a good relationship. Be prepared for returns home when an affair ends, when a marriage or other relationship falls apart, when a job is left, when money is gone or is being saved for a tour of India, Europe or America.

Part 3

Adversity and Diversity

COPING WITH DIVORCE AND DEATH

THE GRIEVING PROCESS IN CHILDREN:

When a parent dies or leaves the family home for good, the children left behind are plunged into deep grief. This chapter looks at that grieving process related to both death and divorce, and at strategies for coping. Regarding permanent separation and death, most grief counsellors agree that the *degree* of grief suffered is influenced by the child's age, personality and previous relationship with the deceased or absentee parent.

Older girls often appear ghoulish (to adults) about the mechanics of death. They ask blunt, awkward questions which should always be answered openly. When describing death don't tell them that someone 'went away'. Euphemisms only confuse children and imply that the dead person can return. In simple language, explain about death being final.

For several years after the father dies or leaves home forever, daughters often insist on sleeping in the mother's bed. Opinions on this practice are mixed, depending on to whom you talk. Obviously it cannot be allowed to continue for *too* long. In order to grow into an adult, the child must be encouraged to sleep alone, but reassured the mother will come if the child calls out. Many mothers have admitted that in those terribly lonely first months of bereavement (or divorce), they found the presence of a child in their bedroom, in what is now a lonely home, of enormous comfort.

The three most common questions asked by young girls when a parent has died or left home for good are:

- 'Did *I* cause Dad (or Mum) to go away?' (Guilt)
- 'Who *else* is going to die?' (Fear)
- 'What do I do if something happens to *you*?' (More fear)

All grieving children need constant reassurance that you, their sole carer, will always be there for them and that they are *in no way* responsible for the death concerned. Many girls whose parents have divorced suffer the same feelings of guilt and unworthiness as those whose parent has died. Sometimes this converts into an eating disorder: 'I was so bad/unattractive it was my fault Dad/Mum left. If I had been prettier/smarter/more lovable, he/she wouldn't have left. So, I'm so bad, I don't deserve food.' This may be the girl's reasoning (see the chapter on eating disorders). If *you* experience problems connected with death or grief, get professional help yourself so that you can steer your daughter through a difficult period.

Share your emotions — cry if you have to. Telling 'white' lies, insisting 'Mum's just fine' when you obviously aren't, helps neither you nor her. Tell her the truth. 'I'm feeling very sad. This sadness might make me cross or anxious at times, but it's *not* your fault. I love you very much and we'll get through this together.'

Be prepared for a range of reactions, varying from tears to anger or total denial. Some girls cope by pretending the death hasn't happened. This is why it is vital for them to attend the funeral, visit the grave, etc. In the case of a parent's death or a divorce where your daughter will not see that parent again, she may panic and search desperately for a substitute, *any* substitute. This can cause intense embarrassment if she asks a family friend of the opposite sex or a casual visitor if he/she plans to become her new Dad/Mum.

Bereaved girls often suffer frightening nightmares, gripped by fear that death may strike again. They need to be reassured, a light left on in their room and you to go to them if they call out. Watch for signs of depression, in yourself as well as in your daughter, and bear in mind grief and depression can be *just* as intense in children as in adults.

Because they may not understand their own feelings, many girls can't release their anguish in words. Asking them to make you a drawing of the dead person *may* help release pent-up grief.

Girls with depression have similar symptoms to adults. They become shy and withdrawn. They lose their appetite and joy in life, sleep badly and often develop strange aches and pains. If you suspect that your daughter is depressed, get professional help. Depression is one of the main factors in youth suicide, and bereavement can act as a trigger, though suicide attempts in teenage girls, usually by an overdose of pills, are often cries for help. Unlike boys, girls rarely use guns when attempting suicide.

BEHAVIOURAL PROBLEMS AFTER DEATH OR DIVORCE

- **Babies** can become 'clingy' and irritable; they may cry a lot or thumb-suck for comfort. (Taping the thumb to the hand with sterile surgical tape is a possible solution to this, although it usually ceases of its own accord after a time). Prolonged thumb sucking could give rise to problems with baby's teeth — consult your dentist if you are worried it has continued too long.
- **Toddlers and preschoolers** are aware of their total dependence on the remaining parent and suffer fear of rejection and abandonment. They may whine when it's time to go off to preschool, regress in potty training, wet the bed, have temper tantrums, lose verbal skills. They can start (or return to) thumb-sucking, refuse to be parted from a 'security' or 'comfort' blanket and hit other children. They cannot comprehend loss and will expect the departed parent to return for birthdays and Christmas.

- **Elementary schoolers** from six to eight years are more pre-occupied with loss, rejection and guilt, unable to understand they are not responsible for the divorce or for the death of a parent. They may have difficulty concentrating and, naturally, their school performance will suffer. They may get stress-related headaches or stomach pains, take out their anger on the custodial parent or, in case of divorce, continue to have hopes of their parents' reconciliation.
- **Pre-teens** from nine to twelve can suffer depression over a dead parent. In the case of divorce, they have a strong sense of loyalty, tend to side with the parent they feel was 'wronged' and turn against the parent who they feel initiated the break-up. At this age exposure to adult TV makes many seem more mature than they really are. They may suffer from stress-related headaches, stomach pains or nervous tics; they may bite their nails, lie, steal or shoplift, wag school or quarrel, hit or bully others.
- **Adolescent girls** react worst of all psychologically. They may become rebellious, get involved with drugs and/or alcohol, play truant, 'drop out' or, searching for a 'father' figure, become sexually promiscuous or enter a disastrous sexual relationship. Naturally, in these circumstances, school performance will suffer. Conversely, girls can also react in a positive way: take over a much more responsible and adult role in the family and 'parent' their younger siblings.

COPING WITH CONFLICT AND HOSTILITY

Girls who cope best after their parents' divorce are those who continue to see *both* parents. Children are bound to grieve when one of their parents leaves the family home forever and must be reassured that they will see him or her again. Give them a calendar on which they can mark the next access visit and look forward to that date. Where a divorced parent renounces visiting rights or simply disappears, the loss to the child and the grieving process can be similar to that occurring after a death. The 'bolter parent' causes great suffering too. 'Bolters' promise to send cards and Christmas presents but never keep their promises, so the child becomes distraught.

The greater and more prolonged the conflict over a separation or divorce, the more severely it can affect your daughter. She needs to maintain a good relationship with *both* parents, even though you may loathe each other. Disputes over money and who has custody can harm your daughter in the long term. If there are disputes of that nature, they should *not* be discussed in her presence. It doesn't help to play 'goodies and baddies'. Asking your daughter to take sides or making the other parent seem a monster is unfair to her. On the other hand, if you praise the other parent too much, she may well ask, 'Well then, why *did* you break up?'

Be aware that instability, change, parental conflict and divorce or death affect children badly and make most kids dread further changes.[1] This may not be easy, but try to keep the same recreations and social contacts and, if at all possible, try not to change your daughter's school at this difficult time.

SHARED WORRIES CAN DRAW YOU CLOSER TOGETHER

The problem is that, after divorce or bereavement, your disposable income usually changes and can affect how (as well as where) you live. Even if you do not want it, your children may have to change schools and leave friends behind. The situation, if explained properly, can draw you closer together, united in surviving as a family unit.

Dr Janet Irwin's distinguished career in medicine has been dedicated to helping women achieve their full potential. She believes that divorce drew her children close to her.

My three children are baby boomers, a first-born son and two daughters, all born within three years. I married against my father's wishes at the age of twenty, when studying medicine at university in New Zealand, but dropped out in fifth year, when I had babies. For over a decade I worked hard at mothering my children, sewed for the family and made all the girls' dresses. My mother was a great support at this time, as she was when I got divorced. She was never judgmental. She mothered by instinct.

When my children's father eventually left us, they were aged fourteen, thirteen and eleven. My divorce, when it came, was a great relief for all of us. We had just enough money to get me through medical school, which **I could not have done without the support of my children.** The following three years were the busiest and hardest of my life, but it was a matter of survival and the best option for me. I *had* to earn enough to support all four of us.

The children were fully involved in all major family decisions and purchases. After their grandfather died, leaving money to pay for their education, they went off to boarding school without a fuss. I didn't like them going away, but boarding school did make them independent. They learned to get on well with other people, and being away from home taught them to appreciate it and took much of the 'sting' out of their adolescence. I worked on the wards as a house surgeon and had long, irregular hours. When the girls were home they did the washing, ironing and cooking, and cared for the dog.

I went to Edinburgh for work and postgraduate study when the girls were in their late teens, and they spent a year with me in Scotland before I returned to New Zealand. Later I accepted a job in Australia as head of a busy university medical centre. Now that I am retired from full-time medicine, the girls and I live in the same Australian city and are close. We share many friends and enjoy the experience of cooking for them together.

Of course, 'letting go' is never easy, especially for the single parent. Adolescents leave but often return later. The important thing is to keep an open door and let them come back if they want to. Experience has taught me if you really want to *keep* your children, you must first let them go.

♥ A Real-life Story ♥

HOW *you* CAN HELP

COMING TO TERMS WITH DIVORCE

- Explain to your young daughter that after many years people can find it hard to live together, so they fight. Now you think it's better that you live apart.
- If possible, your divorce arrangements should include fixed times for her to phone the non-custodial parent and for access visits.
- Spend as much time as possible with your daughter and be generous with physical contact. But don't allow yourself to be manipulated into spoiling her. When you say 'no' on questions of discipline, really mean it.
- If your daughter misbehaves, don't criticise, belittle or ridicule her. She *needs* clearly defined limits and routines. If your daughter is still quite young, don't let the divorce disrupt her routine too much. Children are creatures of habit. Routine gives security and comfort to your daughter at a time when her security and stability are threatened by change and loss.
- Reaffirm *your* house rules, which may be different from those of your ex-partner. Talk to other divorced parents, see what problems they are experiencing and learn from them.
- If you had a good relationship with your in-laws before your divorce, try to continue seeing them now for your daughter's sake, especially at birthdays or Christmas, when she will most miss the other parent. Ask them to send your daughter cards and be involved in her life. Failing this, find a suitable person (relative, teacher, sports coach, housekeeper) to act as substitute carer in addition to yourself.
- Make her feel needed, capable, competent and much loved. List all the household and other tasks she can take over from you.
- Don't use your daughter to convey messages about money to the other parent or to 'snoop' on him/her to see how much money is coming into their household. However aggrieved you may feel, *don't* blame the other parent in front of your daughter. If you feel very hostile, avoid meeting when he/she comes to collect her.
- Never, never flirt with your daughter's boyfriend, it will make you look stupid in her eyes and will cause a rift between you.

GOING SOLO – SINGLE PARENTHOOD

BRINGING UP YOUR DAUGHTER SINGLE-HANDED

Records show that during the year 1996, 52,466 divorces were granted to Australians and 10,009 to New Zealanders.[1] A university study reveals that one in every two marriages now ends in divorce. Many second marriages with children involved break up within five years.[2] As a result, a high proportion of children worldwide are now living with blended families or single parents.

The stigma has been removed from divorce; divorcees are no longer outcasts as they were a century ago. This has benefited many who were locked into unhappy marriages, but has encouraged the belief that, when the going gets tough, one partner should leave. The result is that larger numbers than ever of determined, caring parents, divorced and widowed, have been parenting children on their own. Many of these single parents work extremely hard and deny themselves a great deal in order to provide stable and loving environments for their children and to give them all the support necessary. Everyone knows cases of devoted single mothers and fathers who have sacrificed their own chances of a second relationship and channelled love and energy into raising their children.

Cases of men as single parents are rarer, as mothers usually get custody. In the following sad but true story of a single father's devoted love and care, all names have been changed.

A Real-life Story

A SUCCESSFUL SINGLE FATHER

At Christmas 1975 four couples went camping together on a beach on beautiful, unspoiled Stradbroke Island. Five years later, all four marriages had ended in tears and divorce. The youngest of the couples, Mark and Marianna, had met on a trip to England and fallen in love. At the time Mark did not know that Marianna had had a troubled childhood as a result of her parents' divorce. Mark, who was intending to enter the priesthood, renounced his vocation for her.

Mark switched from theological studies to psychology, married Marianna and had a baby. The young couple were befriended by one of the older couples they got to know well on that camping holiday. Lance, a respected senior lecturer in clinical psychology at Queensland University Medical School, was supervising Mark's postgraduate thesis. At Mark's request, Lance (going through his own mid-life crisis) treated Marianna for postnatal depression. Several psychiatrists in the medical school became worried, knowing that Lance was far too close to Marianna to be able to treat her objectively as a patient. Meanwhile Lance's kind-hearted wife often cared for Mark and Marianna's adorable baby girl Josie, so that Marianna could have a break away from the pressures of parenting and help her conquer her bouts of postnatal depression.

Unfortunately, Lance abused his professional role of trusted psychological counsellor as well as friend of the young couple. After a lengthy series of treatment 'sessions', he ran away with Marianna (who was only a few years older than his own daughter), causing a university scandal. Poor Mark, in a state of shock, was left to bring up baby Josie on his own. Lance's middle-aged wife, shocked and distraught, attempted suicide but eventually recovered. Their only daughter, badly affected by the divorce and by her mother's attempted suicide, 'dropped out'.

Mark and little Josie moved to another city, where he devoted himself to his career and to raising his beloved daughter very well indeed. Josie modelled herself on her father, studied hard at school and university, graduated in medicine and is now a general practitioner. She refuses to have anything to do with her mother, who is widowed and lonely after Lance died. Josie can never forgive the fact that her mother selfishly destroyed *two* marriages.

Now Mark plans to hand over his house to Josie. He will finally do what he planned to do before he met and married the beautiful Marianna: enter the Catholic Church, where he hopes to find peace.

SINGLE MOTHERS TRIPLED WORLDWIDE FROM 1960-1992

This group is now so diverse that it is impossible to generalise or draw any firm conclusions about single mothers. The group includes divorcees, women who have separated from their husbands, mothers (often with good jobs) who have chosen to bring up babies without a live-in father, widows on a pension or superannuation pay-out with dependant children, school-age and other mothers supported by a pension and lesbians without live-in partners, who have had a baby by artificial insemination.

Contrary to all the criticism about single mothers, most are only on a pension for an average of three years. They cope well, raise children who do them great credit.

The group who find single motherhood *least* satisfying are immature young girls.[3] Sadly, many of these girls have no time or motivation for further education or access to it, so they miss out on skilled employment and remain on welfare. These girls are often alienated from their own parents and seldom receive emotional support from their child's father. Among those fully investigated and substantiated cases of neglect or child abuse, 51% take place among this group. These immature single mothers smoke far more than most married mothers and tend to complain that being a lone parent is demanding and stressful.[4] Government reports cite high rates of child abuse and neglect among young single mothers on welfare, often where short-term de facto partners, alcohol and domestic violence are involved.[5] The group with most difficulties are school-age mothers struggling with limited finances. Many had no idea of the work involved in raising a child. They feel isolated from their friends and their children often have behaviour problems.

Unfortunately, TV 'soapies', written for the teenage market, make it look easy for an unmarried schoolgirl to raise her baby alone. The script writers often write in an unmarried mother (played by some beautiful actress), who appears to have a substantial, unearned income and a wardrobe of designer clothes. This fictional character has loads of friends of both sexes, never worries about money or baby-sitters. She is a very poor role model indeed. It is absolutely vital that a young girl, who makes a decision to bring up a child as a single parent, is not basing her expectations on some mushy TV series set in Never-Never-Land. The pregnant girl must be well-informed and know just what she is letting herself in for. Schools, in which a high proportion of pupils are now sexually active, should stress in motherhood classes that babies need to receive love rather than give it back, that single parenting by anyone, school age or mature, can be extremely stressful, particularly when money is short and accommodation is substandard, or when the child develops severe health problems.

A realistic account of surviving as a single mother on a government pension is contained in *Just Me and the Kids,* by divorcee Diana Kupke, who describes her own stress and loneliness.[6] She writes about the difficulties of budgeting on a pension and advises how single mothers can pare expenses to the bone. She also warns isolated parents against getting onto addictive tranquillisers when stress overwhelms them. Kupke describes how a continually crying or screaming child can drive *anyone* to rage and despair. Whenever she felt like hitting her children (as when her toddler poured an entire bottle of nail varnish on her only good dress) she vented her rage by doing the ironing rather than risk battering her children.

Working in a child and family therapy clinic in a British military hospital in Germany, decades ago, the author of this chapter was surprised to hear many stressed-out young mothers recounting their fears that they might take violent action against continually crying babies and hyperactive toddlers, who they described as 'unmanageable'. Patients in this clinic were young British Army wives whose husbands spent long periods away on military exercises. They were, to all intents and purposes, single mothers, living in isolation from their families in rented high-rise accommodation and in a strange country whose language they did not speak. The rate of battered children was high, as was abuse of tranquillisers and suicide attempts by these unfortunate women. Sadly, as soon as our team (social worker, psychologist and consultant psychiatrist) discovered evidence of battering, the mother withdrew the child from treatment. No legislation existed to make them attend the clinic for support, counselling and/or therapy.

Another difficult situation is when an adolescent demands to live with the other parent full-time. Complex emotions about possession and jealousy must be addressed by the parent who feels abandoned. Children have a deep need to love each divorced parent, no matter what sins have been committed. If spouses and ex-spouses have reached the stage where they can talk once again, it makes things much easier. Remember, kids may explore the idea of living with one or the other parent, but still wish that both parents remain in their lives.

Problems arise when the non-custodial parent seeks to 'buy' the child's love with expensive presents and Sunday outing treats, leaving the other parent with all the routine hassles: the school runs, dental appointments and crisis management of adolescent moods.

'Splitting' divorced parents is a well-known syndrome at which many daughters excel: 'But Dad/Mum always lets me do xxx — why don't you?' becomes a catchcry. Faced with this situation, the benevolent (usually living-away) parent must relinquish the 'spoiling' role, or trouble will ensue. Many parents are blind to their own behaviour and it may take an experienced intermediary to present the situation clearly when parenting routines change. It is vital to come to an agreement in advance and talk through issues affecting the child's future.

THIS COULDN'T HAPPEN TO ME... OR COULD IT?

Bullying and harassment of single parents (and sometimes married mothers) by teenage children (particularly those who are larger and more powerfully built than their mothers) is another late twentieth-century hazard. This problem is encountered by family doctors, priests, counsellors, psychiatrists and many parents' support groups, who attempt to help parents struggling with this relatively new syndrome. As family breakdowns soar and resident partners are frequently away on business, working longer hours to keep their jobs, the mother may be left in sole charge for weeks on end. Teenagers sometimes exploit the situation for their own ends. Often a teenage brother and sister join together to bully Mum.

Girls wound and bully with words, making scathing remarks about Mum's social, verbal and parenting skills. Most parents (single or not) are far too embarrassed to tell relatives or friends they are being bullied and losing the battle over discipline. So parents keep up a brave front, pretend nothing is wrong and suffer in silence. Issues reported by doctors and counsellors over which teenagers harass and bully their parents are:

- The right to more pocket money or consumer goodies, with kids claiming 'everyone else's' parents provide more than they get. One solution to this is to ask your child to produce six 'everyone elses' with phone numbers, whose parents can be phoned for confirmation. It's usually impossible to produce them!
- Demands to relax late-night television viewing or party curfews (because 'everybody else' is allowed to, so *why* can't I/we?). See above about producing six parents of the mythical 'everybody'.
- Modes of dress, pierced bodies and outrageous hairstyles.
- The right to bring home sleazy or dope-addicted kids, whom the parent considers highly 'unsuitable' and has told the child so.
- Taking over the kitchen and sitting room when entertaining school friends or throwing wild parties where alcohol and marijuana are available. This sort of behaviour, once deemed unthinkable, is now increasing worldwide, according to family therapists and various parents' support groups who try to help.

PARENTAL BURN-OUT:

In most cases the mother is deeply ashamed, feels it is *her* fault for 'not bringing them up properly' and does not like to tell adult friends or other family members that she is being bullied. Since recent studies indicate that as many as 20% of families do not have the children's father living with them for long periods, due either to divorce or the father's business commitments, it often becomes difficult for the sole mother to get male support to discipline kids.

We have greatly extended the period of education and training required to assume an adult role in our changed technological society, so many kids now stay at home far longer. Before tertiary education became widely available and teenage unemployment soared, adolescence was, out of sheer necessity, brief. Fifteen- or sixteen-year-olds went out to work as apprentices and felt they played some kind of role in society, however humble. Today most stay home until their early or even late twenties. Some leave home and, finding the going tough and phones costing money, ping-pong back, often laden with consumer goods. Others face the unnerving and depressing prospect of *never* finding a worthwhile job. Some are unsure of the future (consciously or subconsciously) and fear they may never be able to have a lifestyle similar to their parents'. So they demand that you, the parent, buy them the electronic toys and designer clothes and footgear they see advertised. This can lead to parental burn-out and disillusion. Pubescent girls, subject to hormonal imbalance and mood swings, experience fluctuating moods and tantrums. By now they know only too well how to wound their mothers by criticising their dress sense, blaming them for a marriage breakup, etc. Kids may have experienced domestic violence in their parents' (broken) marriage. Rows between parent and teenager may end up as screaming matches involving pushing, shoving and other violent behaviour.

A single parent, feeling guilty over marriage breakdown and the child's bitter sense of deprivation and parental loss, hesitates to blame her child. 'Oh, it's just Jan in one of her moods!' is a familiar excuse heard by health professionals. The danger is that in a Catch-22 situation, the aggressive behaviour sets up a pattern for the future. Working longer hours so you can give more money to the problem child or children is no substitute for your time and certainly doesn't make their aggressive behaviour vanish.

SORROW. Lithograph by Vincent van Gogh
Rijksmuseum Vincent van Gogh, Amsterdam

POINTS TO REMEMBER

- If parents give in to teenagers' aggressive demands, just to 'get some peace', the children's offensive behaviour will only escalate. If you give your children everything *they* want, you may have to work extremely hard to fulfil their demands, and parental burn-out could well be the consequence.
- Teenagers may become abusive, or even aggressive, if their demands are thwarted. Some mothers, who try to avoid rows, tend to give in to their children's wishes. In particular, single mothers (or mothers left on their own for long periods) are often victims of their children's excessive demands or emotional blackmail.
- Parental burn-out is increasing among parents who desperately want their children to love them. Many do everything around the house themselves, instead of requiring their children to contribute to household duties. These parents work hard to give them holidays, nice clothes, computers, stereos, CD players and videos — all the things kids see advertised and wish to possess. Believing they are doing 'the right thing', these parents fail to set limits, instil responsibility or apply appropriate punishments, hoping to be 'pals' with their children.
- Don't let your daughter bully *you*. Stand up for yourself. Talk in a deeper voice than normal and *sound* firm (even if you don't feel it). Say, 'Every family is different. I am not X's mother. I/we don't do this because...' Adolescents need to know where you, as a parent, draw the boundaries.
- If you can't cope when your daughter bullies you, either physically or uses foul 'gutter' language, and makes unreasonable demands, contact an adult male relative, friend, counsellor or family doctor to support you. If your daughter is out of control and you are at the end of your tether, don't be ashamed of admitting it. You could also find support by joining a suitable parents' support group, such as Tough Love Parents' Support Group.

SURVIVING THE BLENDED FAMILY

THE BLENDED FAMILY

In her popular novel, *Other People's Children*, author Joanna Trollope, a stepmother herself, predicts that by the year 2010 there will be more blended or step-families than 'birth-families'.[1] Blended families will soon be the norm.[2] Anyone taking on stepchildren should read Joanna Trollope's novel as a cautionary tale. She views blended families as hotbeds of conflicting emotions.

Other People's Children explores the jealousies and rivalries of wives and ex-wives as well as the insecurities and rivalries of their children and stepchildren. Joanna Trollope's characters teach us a great deal about ourselves and the complexities of modern living at a time when nearly half of all second marriages end in divorce. A higher percentage of de facto partnerships fail once children from previous relationships are involved. It must be remembered that stepchildren are struggling to find a place for themselves in a new order which *they* have not chosen. In blended (or not-so-blended) families, life can be a tangled web of rivalries, jealousies and insecurities, in which children find their parents' renewed interest in sex 'gross' or even 'absurd'. In Trollope's novel, as in real life, embittered first wives set their children against stepmothers, who are trying hard to 'do the right thing'.

In today's world blended families are all around us. However, not all stories of blended families are unhappy. Especially in the case of a child whose birth mother has died, a close bond can develop between her and the stepmother.

Two of the contributors to this book are step-parents to large and successfully blended families. Step-parenting *can* be rewarding and successful, but it is *not* the same as mothering. Never forget that even if *you* teach stepchildren to walk, read, swim or ride, you are always 'the stepmother', never their 'real mother'. The real-life story of Jenny and Ian at the end of this chapter is only one of many where expectations of blending two very different groups of children into one family were, unfortunately, too high. Due to the additional stresses of raising stepchildren (and, in many cases, the stepmother also working hard to hold down a responsible job), divorce rates in second marriages have soared to some 47%.[3]

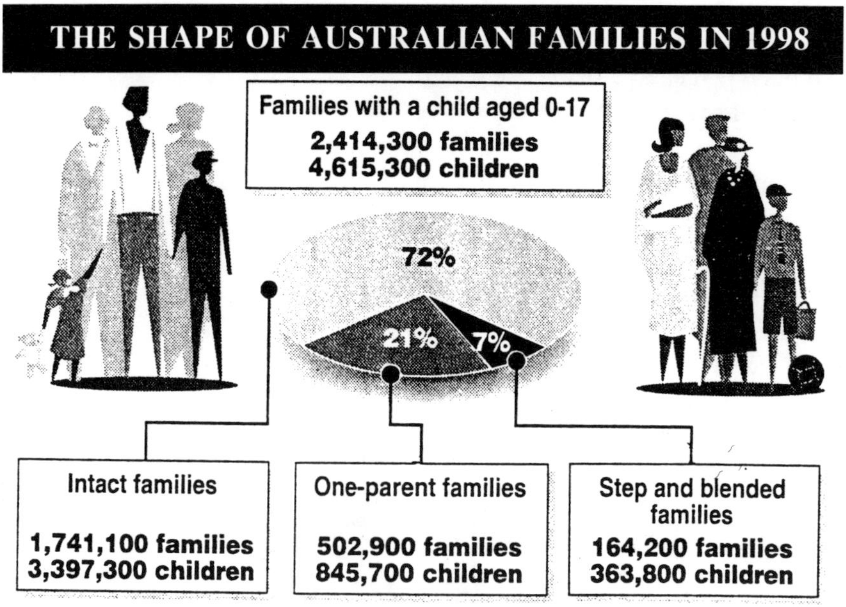

Published in 'The Australian', 23 April 1998

'Wicked' stepmothers (and stepfathers) have traditionally been villains in fiction, like the wicked stepmother in Snow White. On the other hand, step-parents often expect *too much* of stepchildren, who, of course, haven't bonded to them as babies. Remember, love and bonding don't come instantly and there's still a lot of baggage around from the past. If you, as a step-parent, view them as 'foster children' in need of love, rather than 'birth children' bound to you by nature and nurture, then you won't be disappointed if they initially keep you at arm's length. Often they have been encouraged to view you as the 'scarlet' woman who 'stole their Dad'. However, in many cases this situation can change with time. When they eventually leave the comforts of home and have to fend for themselves, they may realise just how much you did for them and may eventually send you a card on Mother's Day.

Although for some lucky and very tolerant people second marriages do work, it's *never* easy and needs enormous flexibility on all sides. Many stepchildren act out their (and their mother's) despair and rage over 'losing' a parent by resenting the step-parent. Trying to win potential stepchildren over by hugging and kissing them at your first meeting will have just the opposite affect. Take things slowly. It might be a good idea, before considering a second marriage with stepchildren involved, to consult a relationship counsellor or attend a course in conflict resolution.

The damage that happens to children when parents separate stems not so much from the actual parting of the mother and father, but from the *hostility* that can continue between the pair of them, in which children (the passed-around generation) are used as pawns.

Negative and bitter feelings about a failed marriage must be set aside. There may be no clear-cut rights and wrongs but rather a series of options for the future, each with positive *and* negative elements, which need to be discussed between partners.

The difference between parenting your own children and stepchildren is *huge*. In second marriages one partner has in a manner of speaking 'shopped around' for a new spouse, but *not* for a new child. This parent may have totally unreal expectations of a relationship with the child, so tensions are created. Some stepchildren feel so threatened by what they see or fear as loss of love that they can be openly hostile, often urged on by non-custodial parents who do not wish their partner's second marriage to succeed. Stepchildren often deny their anger and can appear loving, but later reveal hostility in a number of spiteful ways, or become extremely depressed. A few depressed stepchildren attempt 'cry-for-help' suicide, designed to draw attention to their plight.

Your blended family may *seem* to outsiders like a nuclear family, but reality is nearly always different. The 'wicked step-mother' myth lingers on. Most teenage girls are less than delighted at the idea of a live-in stepmother. They have grown up fast and may have been doing some of the cooking, while Dad has been alone. They may not fancy letting another woman into 'their' kitchen and their life. They may, like Samantha and Chrissie in our story, have been spoiled by their father so won't welcome *anyone* with ideas on discipline. Girls' reactions to a new stepmother are linked to their personality, their age, their friends and their relationship with the non-custodial parent. Some turn their feelings inward and are overwhelmed by sadness, others lash out at the stepmother, who they believe to be responsible for their family breakup, and refuse to admit her good points.

If you and your new partner are joined by stepchildren or a child from your previous marriage, try to identify potential difficulties and talk through them together. If your new partner is diffident or even hostile about taking in your daughter on a long-term basis, then you should think carefully whom you value most, the new partner or your child. Some young daughters are desolate at not having a father-figure around, so much so that when a man arrives to repair the fridge or deliver milk, they can demand, to your embarrassment, 'Are you going to move in and be my new Dad?' When a divorced mother acquires a boyfriend or remarries, her daughter sees Mum flirt with him, buy new clothes and become sexier. Adolescent daughters often crave male admiration. They can practise flirting on Mum's new lover or husband, sometimes with dramatic and tragic consequences.

HOW *you* CAN HELP

- Don't be discouraged by stepchildren who misbehave or are rude. Take things slowly. Keep a dialogue going.
- Talk over potential problems with both sets of children and involve them in major decisions. Treat stepchildren and your own the same, no matter *how* they behave. Help them cope with change and suppressed anger.
- You must set ground rules, including ringing home if any child will be out past supper time and will miss a meal. To avoid rows insist, 'If *you* come in late, *you* heat up or microwave the food I have prepared and *you* clean up afterwards.'
- Develop a parenting and access plan with your new partner. Any plans work better if the non-custodial partner agrees to stick to ground rules about access visits or weekends away. When children are going on such visits, give them appropriate clothes and toys. Make sure they are on time. It makes things easier to have a few rules which are agreed upon by all of you, including, if possible, your stepchildren's mother. Such an arrangement minimises the risk of 'splitting' parental authority. Be aware, even these precautions will not prevent children of divorced parents from trying to play off one parent against another.
- Try to include in your new life some relations of your stepchildren, such as uncles, aunts or cousins. It will help with step-parenting and give them much needed continuity in their lives.
- If serious problems arise, seek help from a relationship counsellor, a psychologist or your family doctor. Talking things over with a professional and impartial person will help.
- If you have been married before, *don't* say 'We always did x...' You are now in a *new* relationship: people and situations differ. Explain *why* you have reached certain decisions. Be consistent.
- Don't continually run down the divorced or separated partner in front of his or her children, especially over money. This only causes children short-term distress and possible long-term damage.

A Real-life Story

A STEPMOTHER'S DILEMMA

Jenny, widowed ten years ago, is an efficient and highly organised nursing sister with three daughters. For years she has worked with Ian, a doctor, whose artist wife left him. Ian confided his problems to Jenny, who was a sympathetic listener.

One day Ian invited Jenny to have dinner with him. A week later they made love. After some months of having an secret affair, Ian asked Jenny to marry him. She accepted, sold her small home and she and her three girls moved into Ian's much larger house. Jenny's background is different from Ian's affluent one. For years she has been working hard to raise her kids. Her two younger girls are doing well at a government school while her eldest is at university.

Ian has two pretty, but very spoiled, teenage daughters, Samantha and Chrissie. Before Jenny's family moved in with Ian, all five girls seemed to get on well together. It suited Ian's daughters' party-going habits that their father was staying until late at Jenny's house.

Samantha and Chrissie felt threatened by a resident stepmother and hated seeing their father cuddling Jenny. Rows took place over who should stack the dishwasher, clean up the kitchen and family room after meals. Ian's daughters are untidy, they were never taught to pick up anything after themselves, much to Jenny's despair. She insists Chrissie and Samantha tidy up their bedrooms, 'toe the line' and conform to the way she is raising her own girls.

Chrissie and Samantha remain loyal to Lauren, their mother. Lauren makes them feel daring, grown-up and sophisticated. Her artist friends even smoke marijuana with the girls. When they stay over at her studio, Lauren never cares how much mess they make. Samantha, a spoiled teenage 'ballet princess', rebels against Jenny's rules, urged on by Lauren. Both girls refused to allow Jenny to attend functions at their school with Ian, which hurts her. All Jenny's well-meaning attempts to win them over seem fruitless — she has lost hope her stepdaughters will ever grow to love or even accept her.

The tense situation at home has badly affected Jenny and Ian's marriage and their tempers. Jenny feels 'put upon' and that Ian leaves far too much disciplining to her. He now works longer hours and is frequently away at medical conferences. She fears that she is gradually losing him and has become tense, withdrawn and moody. Will her second marriage survive?

ADOPTED CHILDREN AND THE DONOR DILEMMA

THE PROCEDURES AND PITFALLS OF ADOPTION

Over the past twenty years there has been a 70% rise in numbers of children born outside marriage, yet the number of babies available for adoption has dwindled to a trickle. Today it can take as long as ten years for suitable couples to be allocated an Australian child to adopt; for a child from the Third World it takes between one and two years.[1]

One result of the shift in attitudes, whereby many Australian single mothers keep their children (while it is believed others abort the foetus), is that the majority of babies available for adoption are foundlings or orphans from impoverished families in Third World countries. It is neither a cheap nor an easy procedure to adopt a child from another country: screening of all prospective parents is intensive. Emotionally, the whole procedure can be harrowing for adoptive parents, especially in overseas adoptions from the Third World. Often, these would-be parents see the child they have come to regard as 'theirs' kept in squalid conditions in orphanages.

The rigour of the vetting procedure, the trauma and high cost of adoption, including visits to foreign countries to see the child, tend to winnow out those whose desire to adopt was not very strong, leaving only deeply committed couples to pursue their aim of adopting a child. Detailed investigations of all prospective adoptive parents' health, stability, income and medical history are carried out. No one with a criminal record is allowed to adopt.

With Australian-born babies, a trial adoption period is now mandatory, during which the baby's birth mother can change her mind and reclaim her baby *before* the adoption is finalised in court.

Few adoptive families are known to abuse a child who has been so deeply wanted. In marked contrast, many of the 91,734 cases of violent child abuse and neglect notified to Australian Government authorities in 1996 were children of isolated, single and immature mothers.[2] A report on homicide in Australia, from the

Australian Institute of Criminology, reveals that 'more infants under the age of one year are murdered each year in Australia than die in either motor traffic accidents, accidental poisonings, falls or drownings'. Most of these are victims of ongoing abuse, mainly by immature single mothers or de facto partners.

In spite of many positive findings on adoption, there still remains some pressure on schoolgirls to keep their ex-nuptial babies. Some are told that adoption is cruel and, should they allow it, their baby will grow up disturbed and unhappy. Margaret Evans, widowed mother of a pregnant schoolgirl, told a social worker she was unable to provide vital support if her 14-year-old daughter kept her baby. Catherine, her pregnant daughter, favoured adoption, but was encouraged by a social worker to keep her child or she would be regarded as 'a bad person'. The social worker told Catherine she would get 'heaps of money and support from the Government'.[3] The reality is that the pension for a single mother with one child is scarcely a generous one. It is vital that the decision to relinquish or keep the baby is made by the mother herself, without pressure from social workers.

Schoolgirl mothers, who fear they cannot raise a child properly or prefer to finish their education, can be acting highly responsibly in having an ex-nuptial child adopted. In some cases they appear far more responsible than a pregnant schoolgirl with no job skills and lacking parental support who keeps her baby under poor living conditions, claiming, 'I just want someone to love *me*'.

Adopted babies are deeply wanted. Their parents are mature, love the children and most can give them the advantage of a stable home and a good education. Having riches is not a criterion to be an adopted parent — being stable and valuing education is. Adoption is no longer the horror story of babies torn from doped or intimidated single mothers. The Search Institute of America recently carried out a random study of 700 adopted children, revealing most related well to their adoptive parents, had stable and happy childhoods and did well in later life.[4]

TELLING ADOPTED AND IVF CHILDREN THE TRUTH

Most children born by IVF (in vitro fertilisation) never know the identity of their fathers. In the 1970s some IVF clinics destroyed all their donor files in a cruel violation of human rights.[5] Only the State of Victoria insists that all sperm donors must be prepared to be identified once the child turns eighteen. Although this is a step in the right direction, it is still *far* too late to tell children the truth. Failure of parents to inform an adopted or IVF child about her full genetic history runs the risk that another family member will tell her and put an unpleasant slant on the story, causing more trauma for all concerned. Like all children, an adopted daughter wants to know who she resembles and where her talents come from, so she can relate to the history of her own genes. As all children have the right to know their genetic histories, judges in certain States now make this a condition for granting an adoption.

It is vital to tell an adopted child before the age of five that he or she has been adopted. However, it is impossible to state the exact age this should be done, as each adopted child is different.

Probably, the full reality of the adoption situation will not hit home until your adopted daughter is between nine and thirteen years old. Then she may experience a delayed reaction, become insecure and 'difficult' as the realities behind the concept of 'adopted' and 'illegitimate' sink in. She may play up at school and her passage through adolescence may be a stormy and even insecure one, needing an enormous amount of love and reassurance from parents; the miracle is that many adoptive parents do succeed in giving this to adopted children.

If adopted children are not told their genetic history and how their birth parents are faring, they can be embarrassed when doctors routinely demand medical details about their birth parents in order to assess the likelihood of certain hereditary diseases, such as breast cancer or heart disease. The consequences of *not* telling a child she is adopted or the result of IVF, or telling her far too late in life, can lead to rejection of adoptive parents by the child.

Telling a much-loved child the full truth about parentage can be painful. However, for an adopted or an IVF child to know 'Who *am* I?' is paramount.

Unfortunately, most sperm donors have refused to allow themselves to be identified to their children. In certain cases (see the following real life-story) a birth mother may not wish to meet her baby. Such a meeting must be desired by both parties. Emotionally, it can prove a success and lead to further meetings, which in *no* way devalue the relationship with the adoptive parents. The child must have professional counselling first and the meeting be desired by both the birth mother and her child, rather than initiated by a third party. Some meetings are very successful — others do not follow a 'happy families' scenario and result in unbridgeable gaps between child, birth parent and siblings, and end in disillusion.

Adopted children need to know *why* they were relinquished by their mothers. They may believe that they were rejected by their birth parents because something was 'wrong' with them. They may be insecure and have a deep-seated fear of rejection, which can make their future relationships with the opposite sex difficult.

All children should receive love, a stable home and a feeling of self-worth from parents in order to grow up secure and happy. However, for adopted children, trying to cope with the realisation they have two sets of parents and an uncertain history, a secure and loving upbringing is even more important.

On the next page, Susanna de Vries reveals the story of her own adoption. When compiling this chapter, she was greatly helped by a social worker who told her that many women who relinquished ex-nuptial babies did so not because they did *not* love and want them, but because they were highly responsible and realised they could not give their children the advantages they had enjoyed.

Susanna's first eye contact with her adoptive mother. (Story next pages.)

A Real-life Story

THE SEARCH FOR BIRTH PARENTS

Susanna de Vries discovered that her 'birth' mother was a headmistress in Ireland and her father a famous author.

On my tenth birthday my parents told me I was adopted. I felt that the bottom had dropped out of my world. Growing up in London during World War II, my adoptive mother had a nervous breakdown as a result of our house being bombed. This meant my adoptive father spent a great deal of time with me, took me to museums and art galleries and was, in my eyes, the perfect father. I imagined my birth mother as sad and beautiful, having been forced by her parents to relinquish me for adoption. I longed to find and embrace her. I did not want my much-loved adoptive parents, to whom I owed a great deal, to know this.

Only the name 'Emma X, teacher, born central Ireland', was on my birth certificate. Adoption societies at that period refused to supply details to adopted children. My parents had said that my biological father was a journalist and his last known address Sitges in Spain. I imagined Emma as a pregnant student, my father leaving her to fight Fascism in the Spanish Civil War and dying there. I learned Spanish and won a scholarship to study art history in Spain. For years I studied and worked there, but never found his grave.

Years later, I emigrated to Australia with my husband. Like my biological father, I became an author and journalist. Then my marriage broke up, I became depressed, could not concentrate and developed that horror of all who write for their living, writer's block.

A few years later my adoptive mother died on the operating table and, shortly after that, my beloved adoptive father got cancer. I returned to Britain to nurse him — a few weeks later he died in my arms. Still grieving for my adoptive father, I went through his deed box and found among my adoption papers faded press cuttings about the Hon. Edward Ward, journalist, broadcaster and author (who had meanwhile inherited the Irish title of Viscount Bangor).

My adoption society had withheld information from me during my teenage years. However, laws on birth information for adopted children had changed and now they could reveal that the Hon. Edward Ward had written to them from Sitges in Spain. He had offered to pay my mother's 'lying-in fees', but in return insisted his name must not appear on my birth certificate as my father, as he hoped to work for the then-very-stuffy BBC. The adoption society knew no more about him, but revealed that my birth mother had been the head teacher in Monaghan, a small town in the centre of southern Ireland. I obtained Emma's phone number and rang her home. There was no answer. Finally I contacted the local police, who told me that Emma had died two weeks previously, mourned by the entire town.

A Real-life Story

They put me in touch with the lawyer handling my mother's estate. My call to the lawyer caused consternation: Emma's will was missing and as she appeared on my birth certificate as my mother, I would be entitled to half her estate. The other heir was my half-sister, Maureen, who had never heard of me and flatly refused to believe that Emma, the paragon of the local Anglican Church, could possibly have had an illegitimate child. Our conversation was brief and cold.

Back in Australia I wrote to my half-sister, explaining that I had absolutely no intention of making *any* claim on Emma's estate. I added that blood was thicker than water and that I had no surviving relations, other than her. Years later, after more research, I learned that from my father's four marriages I had two half-brothers: William and Nicholas. William, child of Wife No. 3, would inherit the title of Viscount Bangor. By my father's Wife No. 4, I had a multi-talented half-sister, Lalla Ward, the well-known actress and book illustrator.

On a visit overseas I met Maureen X, also a teacher. She told me that her father had disappeared to Australia with another woman, after Emma had found them in bed together. Poor Emma, under harsh laws then in force, was never able to obtain a divorce.

According to Maureen, I looked much like our formidable mother, patron of so many charities and headmistress of a school. She related details of her own childhood, devoid of many things I had enjoyed. Maureen said wistfully, 'You were the lucky one'. She did not want to tell anyone that our mother had an illegitimate child, not even her own children would know the *whole* truth. She was convinced that, had I found Emma, she would have been angry rather than delighted to see me, her 'paragon of virtue' image destroyed. Maureen's feeling that I was my mother's 'disgrace' was obvious.

My father, author, journalist and eventually a well-known BBC broadcaster, had interviewed my mother when she applied to be head of a Anglican school outside Ireland. He was handsome and charismatic and being divorced from Wife No. 1 (divorce in 1935 being a scandal). He and Emma had an affair and she became pregnant. However, Emma could not obtain an English divorce from a 'missing' husband, while Ireland did not allow a divorce at all. Living 'in sin' was impossible for those with high profiles. Emma had no money and female teachers were poorly paid at that time. She would have lost her job if she had returned to that small Irish town to support Maureen and raise an illegitimate baby.

Fortunately, responsible Emma didn't have me aborted and didn't lose her livelihood. Instead, she chose to have me adopted by loving parents, to whom I owe an enormous amount. Thank you, Emma, I'm deeply grateful that you made the right choice, hard as it must have been.

IF YOUR DAUGHTER IS A LESBIAN

GUESS WHO'S COMING TO DINNER?

Most parents look forward to the announcement that their daughter is bringing 'someone special' home to dinner. So, how would *you* react when that special person turns out to be female? When your daughter and her partner exchange long, lingering looks, you realise with a shock that they are in a lesbian relationship.

Your daughter may have harboured secret doubts about her sexual orientation for years, which you probably refused to acknowledge. Research shows that between 9-14% of parents refuse to acknowledge warning signs that their children could be attracted to those of the same sex or be bisexual.[1] You are now faced with a turning point in your lives. How you, as a parent, will react is vital. Should you condemn Juliet's sexual preference or insult her new partner, you risk a scene that may create resentment between you forever. All your arguments in favour of heterosexuality and 'a normal marriage' will not change Juliet's sexual orientation or decrease her infatuation.

Many parents deal badly with this situation and have 'lost' their daughters for years — some have walked out of the door and never returned. How can you keep Juliet (your much-loved baby, whose photographs in christening robe and school uniform adorn your home) as part of your family? You may not have known any lesbians until now and may have disapproved intensely of lesbianism as a way of life. You will probably be dismayed or even outraged. But pause a moment — is some of your shock and outrage based on sheer selfishness? Perhaps you resent the fact that Juliet will never give you grandchildren (although with artificial insemination, there is a chance she might). Your feelings are bound to be influenced by Juliet's age. If she is less than sixteen, the relationship may be only a passing teenage infatuation or 'crush'. After a while, she and her partner may fight bitterly and break up — this happens in homosexual relationships just as it does in heterosexual ones. After living together, she may realise that a lesbian relationship has the same emotional problems and jealousies as a heterosexual one.

If your daughter is reasonably mature, her love for her female partner is likely to be based on a genuine and lasting sexual preference. She may not have told you (parents are often the last to know), but she could have had lesbian experiences at school. She may have tried heterosexual relationships and found the opposite sex disappointing. In today's world she will have seen many marriages break down, possibly making her cynical about men and heterosexual relationships. Juliet's new relationship may also have been influenced by her peer group. She may be working in an area where lesbianism is a strong part of the work culture, usually one where more women than men are employed.

You are mature enough to know that life has many unexpected twists and turns. Your daughter could change her orientation but is certainly not thinking of doing so at this red-hot moment. She may even be experiencing some doubts herself, just as people do when engaged to be married; right now she certainly will not thank you for voicing your disapproval. How you behave here and now will set the tone of the long-term relationship for all of you. It can take years to undo harsh words spoken in the heat of the moment.

If you truly love your daughter, and she seems to have found a reasonable partner who makes her happy, look on the bright side — at least she is unlikely to get AIDS from her partner. Loving relationships should be spiritual and emotional as well as physical. Hopefully, this is what your daughter and her partner have found. They may have been sharing a house or apartment and you liked her as your daughter's 'friend'. Don't start rejecting or even hating her now because you have become aware of the truth. If you do, you will create a deep division between you and your daughter.

The way you react when Juliet finally plucks up the courage to tell you the truth is vital for your future relationship. If her partner seems stable and has secure employment, she may well have a positive influence on your daughter. Although you want for your daughter what *you* consider best, you have brought her up to make choices and this is *her* choice.

TROUBLESOME RELATIONSHIPS

A Real-life Story

Caroline, an architect, had been deserted by her husband years previously. He ran off with the office bimbo who, after exhausting his savings, left him. Caroline, bitterly hurt, refused to have him back.

Caroline worked hard to send Harriet, the only child of her failed marriage, to an exclusive boarding school while she built her own career. Harriet was a good student, had a brief episode of anorexia but got over it and was accepted into university, where she studied Arts-Law. Mother and daughter were close. Harriet always phoned home at least once a week. Initially, she had kept quiet about her relationship with a married lecturer named Andrew. Eventually, Harriet plucked up courage and told her mother.

Caroline warned her daughter against having a relationship with a much older and married man with seductive charm. Harriet soon discovered that she was part of a pattern. Andy had been chasing female students for years, pretending that he and his wife had an 'open' marriage. At first he played the role of father-figure, enjoying making his students psychologically dependent on him and getting them involved, emotionally and physically. Then, scared, he would break off the affair, explaining to the girl in question that it was 'for the sake of his children'. When he broke up with the fatherless Harriet, she became depressed and bitter about the opposite sex and never seemed at all interested in any of the 'nice young men' to whom her mother introduced her.

One Christmas Harriet came home with an older woman named Wendy, with whom she worked in the public service. They both wore identical black leather coats and gold rings, announced they were deeply in love and that they were buying a house together.

Caroline had suspected *something* for over a year. However, suspecting is one thing and finding out another. Her initial reaction was one of shock and dismay.

A Real-life Story

Her daughter was in her first year of paid employment in the public service. Would her avowed intention to flaunt her gender preferences damage her career? How could she know at this age that she would never change? Caroline voiced motherly concerns. Wendy flew into a violent rage. Harriet, bitterly hurt, told her mother she was bigoted and old-fashioned. Christmas lunch was a disaster. Wendy enjoyed trying to shock Caroline by boasting how she and Harriet spent Sundays in bed together, reading newspapers, making love and doing the rounds of gay and lesbian bars and clubs, the only places where they felt accepted.

In the end, Harriet and Wendy packed their suitcases and departed. For a year, Caroline heard nothing from her daughter. Then one night, out of the blue, Harriet phoned her mother. She told her that Wendy, who had always been very fond of frequenting 'gay' bars and had a drinking problem, had crashed her car whilst very drunk. It was clear that Harriet was experiencing all the problems found in an alcoholic, violent marriage: jealousy, bitter recriminations, accusations of unfaithfulness, tears, more recriminations.

Eventually, Wendy left, flatly refusing to pay her share of the mortgage, leaving phone and heating bills outstanding. Harriet was distraught by the breakup and could not pay the accounts. She called her mother for advice. Caroline's lawyer informed her that Harriet had no legal rights in a lesbian relationship and was not protected by the law. Finally, after Caroline had paid large legal bills, some monies were recovered. Harriet sold the house and moved to a rental apartment.

Harriet still goes to gay and lesbian clubs and bars in the Sydney suburb where she lives. She has a network of friends, at present no one special, but she is hoping to find a more stable lesbian relationship. Caroline works in Melbourne and flies to Sydney to spend weekends with Harriet. These weekends are now pleasant and companionable for both of them.

Caroline is at heart a romantic. She still hopes that Harriet may find a 'nice man' to marry and have children, but realises in her more logical moments that this is unrealistic. Caroline now has heart problems and is thinking of retiring early. She realises that her life may be limited. In the years that remain, she hopes to see Harriet a great deal and have as good a relationship with her and any new (and hopefully more suitable) partner. If she wants to continue seeing Harriet, and enjoy spending time with her, it is no good moralising or disapproving of her chosen way of life.

A Real-life Story

A SUCCESSFUL RELATIONSHIP

Alex and Margaret are members of the Uniting Church. They have a daughter named Sandy and a son named Clive. Alex is an accountant and Margaret works part-time in a restaurant.

Sandy had a troubled school career with a crush on an older girl. She attended university but dropped out and went to live in a commune, which worried her parents. When Sandy left the commune after six months, Margaret helped her daughter move into a rental apartment with another student, Anna, who seemed like a suitable friend for Sandy.

'Bring Anna home for lunch,' Margaret invited. Over lunch Sandy told her parents that she had never been attracted to boys. Then she revealed that she and Anna were deeply in love and intended to spend the rest of their lives together. Both parents were horrified and clearly expressed their feelings. Their religious beliefs made it very hard for them to accept Sandy's way of life.

They lost touch for a year. Clive went overseas to work. Margaret and Alex were grieving for their daughter so badly that they decided to invite Sandy and Anna to spend Christmas with them. The girls gratefully accepted the invitation.

Alex and Margaret did their best to make Anna feel welcome. She revealed that her parents had refused to have anything to do with her again unless she renounced her lesbian relationship. Over the Christmas period they noticed that, as a result of the relationship with Anna, Sandy seemed more domesticated, more mature and less selfish. Her parents were also relieved to learn that she seemed to have found her niche in life by going to art school. She exhibited her work in shows of gay and lesbian art and designed a float for the Gay and Lesbian Mardi Gras.

Of course, the situation remains less than perfect. Margaret, influenced by her religion, cannot accept Sandy's way of life as being 'normal', which annoys Sandy, who desperately wants her mother's approval. Sandy's brother Clive, a macho plumber by trade, is even more disapproving than his parents, so Sandy refuses to speak to him.

Fortunately, Sandy and her parents have a better relationship now: the wounds are healing. Sandy and Anna are definitely an 'item', and Anna is talking about having a baby by artificial insemination. They have promised to visit Margaret and Alex on a regular basis and Sandy takes the time to phone home each week.

HOW *you* CAN HELP

WHEN JULIET TELLS YOU THAT SHE HAS A LESBIAN RELATIONSHIP

- It's hard for you to accept but try to appear tolerant. Telling you has not been easy, yet she *has* been honest. Hopefully, she understands that her revelations are hurting you deeply. If you feel distressed, *don't* show it. It will only make things worse.
- Bear in mind that Juliet's love for you has not diminished. Tell her that you, as parents, love her just as much as before and that you understand the depth of her feelings. Reassure her that she is still your daughter, **nothing will change that**.
- Don't force any disapproval of lesbianism onto your daughter. It's too late. All you can do now is hug her and accept her as she is. She wants you to like her new partner.
- Reassure Juliet that she is welcome to bring her partner home, just as long as she respects the rules of *your* house.
- After this has been made clear, point out gently and firmly that you are being **adaptable and open-minded**. In return, you expect your daughter to be the same. You must both leave lines of communication open. She may have had years of self-doubt and unhappiness; for her to think that her gender preference could ever change is unlikely. Like a new religious convert, she wants to talk in glowing terms about her new way of life and the friends she has found. She thinks in a new way and will *not* be prepared to believe anything different right now.
- Be positive. Look for the good points in your daughter's partner. She must have *some*, or your daughter would not love her.
- Once the situation has settled down, have another talk to your daughter. Point out to her that in a lesbian relationship, should it break up, her rights are not protected by law — she has none of the property rights of marriage. Remember that no relationship in this world is without its complications. If your daughter is young, she has decades ahead of her. Who knows, with time she might change. Oscar Wilde said, 'There is only one thing worse than not getting what you want: and that is getting it.'

Part 4

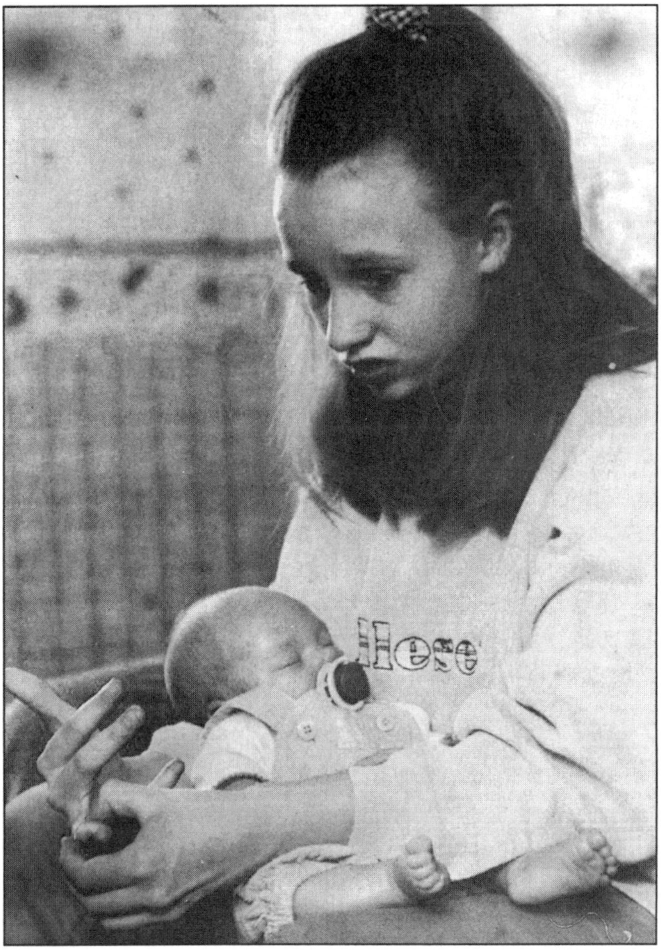

Kathleen — a twelve-year-old schoolgirl with her baby

Parents' Nightmares

SCHOOLGIRL PREGNANCY

WHY DOES IT HAPPEN IN THE AGE OF 'THE PILL'?

Figures for ex-nuptial schoolgirl and teenage pregnancies have more than doubled over the past two decades.[1] Fear of catching HIV-AIDS or the equally lethal Hepatitis B meant 1,000 Australian schoolgirls from government and private schools talked freely about sex to university researchers. The survey revealed that a quarter of all girls in Grade 10 (aged fourteen and fifteen) are sexually active, but less than half of them took the contraceptive pill or used condoms early in the relationship. By the time girls reach Grade 12 (aged around sixteen or seventeen) nearly *half* the class was having sex, usually with someone near their own age. Some 34% of girls in Grade 10 who had sex did *not* insist that the male use a condom because they were too drunk or 'high' to do so; 25.4% of Grade 12 girls having sex were more likely to insist the male partner wore a condom, a higher percentage than girls in Grade 10.[2]

A strong denial factor about schoolgirl sex exists among middle class parents. Most insist *their* daughter is not interested in boys or if she goes out with them is 'so responsible' that she wouldn't have sex. Many parents repeated, 'Yes, I know that xx has sex, but my Juliet isn't like that.' If they discover that their daughter is pregnant, it's red faces and Prozac all round. They fail to understand that the vast majority of schoolgirls today see no moral value in chastity and feel no guilt about premarital sex.

According to the HIV survey, few schoolgirls are aware of the lethal nature of Hepatitis B. Substantial numbers of them use no contraception at all and drink quantities of alcohol before having sex, so it's not hard to understand why they fall pregnant. Teachers reveal that some parents of pregnant girls in private schools or at university, who do not have strong religious beliefs, spend money on abortions in the private sector, fearing pregnancy will ruin their daughter's career prospects. Naturally, these abortions are hushed up. In public schools, pregnancy is usually far more obvious as fewer attempts are made by the parents to conceal the girl's condition. One reason is that a much higher proportion of girls from socioeconomic backgrounds where tertiary education is not seen as essential keep their babies rather than having them aborted. Often Mum valiantly helps out in a time of crisis, takes on extra work (in some cases going out cleaning) and 'mothers' her daughter's baby. Many teenage fathers pay no maintenance and are never seen again once the excitement of the birth is over.

We also have a situation where girls who would once have been pregnant at the altar now refuse to marry the fathers and keep their babies. However, if their parents do *not* help them, some 45% will wind up living with their baby below the poverty line.

A young female hairdresser from a small country town related how three of her sexually active classmates, believing themselves in love with local boys, had permitted the boys to have sex without contraceptives and they became pregnant. Afterwards they discovered that the fathers were 'selfish louts', who had sex with them without love. Although these girls kept their babies, none of them wanted to marry the fathers.[3]

The whole topic is complex: many different factors are involved in today's rate of school-age pregnancies. In her professional capacity, Dr Janet Irwin saw many cases of young girls falling pregnant. After studying the problem for some years she now believes the main factors for school age and student pregnancy are:

- **Sheer ignorance**: Obviously not all schools (and parents) provide enough sex education, or else the message fails to sink in. Dr Irwin once had a pregnant patient who had been trusting enough to believe she could not get pregnant as long as she 'did it' standing up.

- **Contraceptive failure**: Most manufacturers point out that their pill should be taken at the *same* time each day for maximum efficiency. Sex with multiple partners is now a dangerous pastime and the pill gives absolutely *no* protection against life-threatening Hepatitis B, HIV-AIDS or other sexually transmitted infections. Condoms can burst or come adrift during vigorous intercourse. If your young daughter is in a sexual relationship, it is vital that you or her family doctor warn her that *all brands* of the contraceptive pills can fail to prevent pregnancy due to impaired absorption, prolonged vomiting (which means the gut lining fails to absorb the pill) and/or diarrhoea (which causes the same problem). Certain types of antibiotics interfere with the flora that line the gut, which can then prevent absorption of the pill and lead to pregnancy. There are also numerous cases of plain, simple forgetfulness with the pill, especially after a party where alcohol has been consumed.
- **Risk-taking behaviour**: This is seen in teenagers who drive far too fast, take drugs or binge-drink 'for the hell of it' or to act out against their parents. Some young risk-takers have multiple sexual partners. One pregnant thirteen-year-old girl told her general practitioner that it should be relatively easy to identify the father. 'He could only be one of *five* boys I went with,' the girl said without a hint of embarrassment.
- **Denial**: The 'It-may-happen-to-others-but-it-won't-happen-to-me' syndrome. For a variety of reasons teenage girls often fail to use contraceptives when having sex for the first time. Then they start a steady relationship and demand the boyfriend uses condoms. Eventually one or both partners become blasé and feel that while *others* might, *she* won't get pregnant.
- **An overwhelming need for love**: The 'I-desperately-need-someone-to-love-me' syndrome by a girl who feels that a baby would provide closeness and satisfy *her* emotional needs as a living doll. These girls, often the product of broken homes, are emotionally immature and most make very poor mothers.
- **A self-fulfilling prophecy**: One student proudly told Dr Irwin, 'My Mum always says that if I get pregnant, she'll look after the baby.' The result of this statement, oft-repeated, was that the

daughter obliged her mother. Dr Irwin questioned, 'Whose need was it to have a baby — the mother's or the daughter's?'

- **A means of getting financial support**: It is claimed in certain sections of the media that social security benefits and the single parent allowance causes girls, who cannot find jobs, to get pregnant deliberately and keep their babies. Dr Irwin is not sure that these accusations are true and believes that the motivation for pregnancy and motherhood is often a *far* more complex and multidimensional problem.
- **Rape**: A girl may have been raped or consented to intercourse while under the influence of alcohol, sedatives or other drugs.
- **Forceful and/or unreliable sex partner**: A girl may not be able to convince her male partner that he must use a condom, or she may fall for his assertion that it may damage or hurt him if she makes him stop. Many pregnant girls counselled by Dr Irwin told her how they were foolish enough to believe their partner when he promised to withdraw 'in time' (using the technique known as 'coitus interruptus'). Many inexperienced males have not yet acquired the necessary techniques of condom use to ensure maximum safety.
- **Incest**: Young and not very forceful girls may find it impossible to refuse sexual demands from their father, stepfather or close male relative through fear of punishment or the destruction of the family. 'Your mother never lets me. You are the only one who can help me,' the unfortunate girl is told. Father-daughter incest is a frightening mix of the father's abuse of power and betrayal of the father image. It is tragic for the girl's future stability in life when an incestuous relationship of this nature results in a pregnancy that causes guilt to all concerned.

Unlike Britain and New Zealand, Australia's attitude to abortion ensures all States (excepting Western Australia, which is, at the time of writing, changing its legislation) have placed abortion under the Criminal Code rather than the Health Act. Dr Janet Irwin feels strongly that abortion should be removed from the Australian Criminal Code. She asks an important question, 'Are women allowed to make their own major life decisions or are they not?'

WHAT CAN PARENTS DO TO PREVENT PREGNANCY?

Children today obtain information about sex from various sources other than parents: friends, teachers or community-based sex education programs. Casual sex, portrayed in film, TV and magazines, has played a *huge* role in encouraging high-risk sexual behaviour in our society. It's rare today to see a film that does not have a portrayal of sexual intercourse, but condom use is *never* shown. Not one single female character in a film, on the point of having sex, ever says, 'Suppose I get pregnant? Hold on, let's use a condom.' Condom use for health as well as contraceptive purposes does *not* encourage young people to have casual sex. Teenagers do *not* say to each other, 'Wow, here's a condom, let's use it to have sex.'

Remember, parents and daughters can find it difficult to discuss intimate sexual matters *after* puberty. You should regard sexuality as a normal part of life and have an open and honest attitude, which you communicate to your daughter from a young age. With so much emphasis in the media on sex, especially in teen magazines, long before your daughter becomes sexually active, warn her she *must* insist *always* on the boy using contraceptives to protect herself against sexually transmitted infections — and in addition, taking the pill should be discussed with her general practitioner.

WHAT *ARE* THE OPTIONS FOR PREGNANT GIRLS?

Most pregnant girls find it hard to tell their parents, feeling they have 'let them down', fearing parental rejection or punishment. One clergyman's daughter told the truth to her hairdresser and her school friends, but could not tell her parents, so ran away from home. You may suspect that your school-age daughter is pregnant when she becomes moody and tense. Then in tears she reveals she has missed one or two periods. Provided religious principles are not violated, abortion is one possible solution. Always remember, there is *no* single perfect solution to this stressful situation. All possible decisions have outcomes that will cause grief at one stage or another.

A 'shotgun' or forced wedding is seldom seen as acceptable today. A distressingly small proportion of teenage fathers stay around after the child is born. *Any* pregnant schoolgirl *and* her parents have very serious decisions to make about her life, her future and the future of any child she bears. She has to find answers to many difficult questions and consider *all* options. There will be strong feelings on all sides about what to do: relatives may offer different solutions. The final choice must be hers, made in a context of calm and support.

DIFFICULT QUESTIONS

IF YOUR TEENAGE DAUGHTER IS PREGNANT

- Does your daughter want to keep the baby or does she want an abortion? If she loathes the idea of abortion but doesn't want to raise a baby alone, what about today's type of 'open' adoption, where the child grows up knowing the birth mother *and* adoptive parents, as one possibility?
- What is to be done if your daughter wants an abortion but you want her to keep the baby or *vice versa*?
- Does she have the necessary maturity to cope with a crying baby and sleepless nights or with an active toddler, all by herself? If the answer is no, can she rely on *your* full parental and financial support to help raise her baby? Can she afford to rent decent living accommodation, or are you willing to provide a suitable dwelling, transport for her and her child, baby-sit, help with feeding, toilet training, etc. All this is time-consuming. Do you have the time *and* the energy to do this at your stage of life?
- Will keeping her baby put an end to your daughter's education (either secondary or tertiary) or her job training and, consequently, jeopardise her future and that of her child?
- Fathers often desert young single mothers once the novelty has worn off, leaving them desperately lonely. The Australian Institute of Criminology's report on homicide points out the dangers to babies from immature de facto partners who seek a sexual relationship with the mother but don't accept her baby. The report reveals that, in Australia, each year more infants under the age of one are murdered by de facto partners than die in car accidents, accidental poisoning or drowning. Before these babies died, many had endured severe physical abuse, including broken limbs.

FINDING UNBIASED PROFESSIONAL HELP

Probably you and your daughter will spend anxious hours discussing her problem but fail to arrive at a clear decision, so both of you may need professional help. Where can you find it? Some pregnant girls find their own way to a counselling service without the knowledge of their parents. However trained counsellors usually advise *all* girls under sixteen to tell their parents when they are pregnant. Parental consent is essential if an abortion under general anaesthetic is to be performed on these young girls.

If your daughter is in need of professional help, she should go to a sympathetic family doctor or make contact with a Women's Health Centre or Family Planning Clinic. It is *your* responsibility to encourage her to do this. Ideally the doctor or the agency should hold a multidimensional view, *without* putting any pressure on your daughter. A doctor or agency that does *not* consider an abortion as an option, can only recommend continuation of the pregnancy and may offer counselling and short-term support. However, such agencies (often motivated by religion) rarely offer vital support after the birth, when the need is greatest for an inexperienced young and single girl attempting to mother a child on her own.

ABORTION REFERRAL AGENCIES

Abortion imposed by parents or the father of the young girl's child is likely to have long-term adverse emotional consequences. Remember that an abortion imposed on a pregnant girl because someone *else* has a problem about her pregnancy is *not* a good solution. Similarly, continuation of a pregnancy when termination is refused has been shown to have bad long-term effects on both mother and child. An abortion referral agency will give information about available services. The girl will be offered counselling to help her decide whether to continue with the pregnancy or to have it terminated. In New Zealand, as in Britain, laws relating to abortion are liberally interpreted, making specialist abortion clinics available. In Britain a broad interpretation of the phrase 'health of the mother' is enshrined in the Abortion Act of 1967. In both these countries it is legal to perform an abortion when two doctors certify that, in their opinion, continuing the pregnancy would adversely affect the woman's health. In most States in Australia abortion is still in the Criminal Code, but by taking advantage of case law, abortion is usually available, although often not provided in public hospitals.[4]

ADOPTION – HER DECISION ONLY

Some responsible schoolgirl mothers do not want to raise a child alone on a fairly meagre pension if their parents will not or cannot help. They want their baby to have a stable home and good educational opportunities, and realise they cannot provide these. Others, planning tertiary education, do not wish to raise the child themselves, but have strong moral or religious objections to abortion. In such cases, 'open adoption', where the child has continuing contact with the birth mother (or adoption by a married sister or close relative), can mitigate emotional problems for a relinquishing mother. Considering that there are many stable, suitable parents, longing to adopt, 'open' adoption does present a workable solution in many cases, as long as *no one* pressures the single mother into it.

Today's pressure tends to be in favour of schoolgirl mothers keeping their child, even though some thirteen- and fourteen-year-old girls are manifestly incapable of taking care of *themselves* and want their babies adopted.[5] If social workers urge young schoolgirls to raise children alone, they ignore that government statistics reveal that 51% of single mothers and their babies live below the poverty line and that the rate of neglected and abused babies among this group is high. Schoolgirl mothers without full parental support are left feeling isolated and alienated and often cannot cope well. If a pregnant schoolgirl decides to keep her baby, she needs to be made aware of *all* the facts, including just what expenses a pension will cover, the hard work and sacrifice involved in raising a child and how she will need support from her parents for many years. The most important point is that the girl herself feels *she* owns the final decision, whatever it may be.

EATING DISORDERS

'HELP, I'M FAT!' — OBESITY AND CRASH DIETING

Eating disorders and compulsive dieting dominate the lives of 65% of teenage girls.[1] At any one time (according to the Australian National Health Survey) some 42% of all girls aged nine and over are on diets, ranging from total fasts to the so-called Israeli Army diet, which weakens most dieters so much they are highly unlikely to wage war. These girls lose weight as their bodies employ defences that humans have used throughout history to counteract effects of famine. After stopping the diets, their systems go into overdrive and very often they put all the lost weight back on. One in every eight dieting girls can develop an eating disorder.

Girls today are bombarded and confused with conflicting messages about body shape and food. Photos of razor-thin 'smacked out' fashion models adorn magazine pages and are pinned up around the walls of girls' bedrooms. Advertisements in the same magazines, or on commercial television, promote fast-food chains which offer fattening milk shakes, double burgers and 'chips with everything'. Small wonder some girls, under stress or unhappy at home, become compulsive eaters and either suffer from bulimia or become obese. Like other addicts, the obese cannot help overeating, hate themselves for it, then rush to the fridge to eat 'comfort foods' to erase their feelings of guilt and depression. Obesity places the compulsive eater at risk of heart disease and other health problems. It is vital for the future health of obese girls to see a doctor or nutritionist. They can also be helped by well-established diet control groups such as Weight Watchers. Extreme cases, in whom obesity presents serious health risks, may eventually have to be hospitalised for procedures as drastic as stomach stapling.[2]

ANOREXIA AND BULIMIA — FEMININE OBSESSIONS

These are obsessions, caused by deep-seated psychological problems. For widely varying reasons anorexics hate food or feel unworthy of it and embark on programs of self-inflicted starvation.

Often perfectionists, they are convinced that when they become thin, true happiness will be theirs. Anorexia is a very complex disorder with a wide variety of causes. Some anorexics seek to control parents, relatives and friends through food refusal. Others feel guilt over a past event and punish themselves by rejecting food, determined to become skeletally thin. Due to lack of body fat, many anorexics never menstruate, don't develop breasts and can suffer premature osteoporosis, because they do not get sufficient calcium. Side effects include cardiovascular disease and vitamin deprivation, which causes mood swings, loss of hair and insomnia.

Reasons for anorexia are as varied as the stories of those who suffer from it. Some girls can suffer eating disorders as a result of migrating from the Third World to a new country, being exposed to a relaxed way of life at school, but treated in a rigid and patriarchal way at home. When these girls seek to dress in a more casual way, go out or fall in love with 'Westernised' boys, they often encounter strong parental disapproval, which can lead them to stop eating as a way of revenge on their parents. Divorce or death of a parent can also trigger an eating disorder. Victims of oral sexual abuse or rape often convert their feelings of revulsion into a hatred of eating, which involves swallowing. Girls suffering deep-seated psychological problems for *any* reason at all can become bulimic or anorexic. Today girls as young as ten are being hospitalised for these illnesses.

PUBERTY. Detail of painting by Edvard Munch. National Gallery, Oslo.

Bulimics are usually girls with an obsessive love-hate relationship with food. They try to beat fat by dieting or becoming gym and exercise 'addicts'. When the strain of crash-dieting and constant exercising becomes too much, the bulimic finds relief in bingeing on 'comfort' foods, especially ice-cream and custard, which are easy to vomit up. Junk foods provide the comfort the bulimic craves in her efforts to obtain release from stress and tension. By now, she knows that consuming junk foods will make her put on weight, so she induces vomiting by sticking two fingers down her throat. Over time, compulsive and frequent vomiting will destroy the natural movement of food down the oesophagus. Bulimic vomiting can become a reflex action, which will, in time, damage the sufferer's intestines.

Bulimics are deeply ashamed of their solitary and bizarre vomiting, so refuse to admit it to doctors, friends and family. Some worry about damage to tooth enamel and lips and switch to herbal or patent slimming pills, containing herbal laxatives. Others take diuretics, which make them urinate frequently. Some bulimics take up to ten doses of laxatives a day, ensuring their bodies do not retain essential nutrients, vitamins or minerals, with disastrous long-term consequences to their bodies and their moods. Finally bulimics have to seek medical advice when they vomit up blood or suffer crippling stomach pains. They envy anorexics for rapid weight loss, but are unable to starve themselves. They need food. Bulimics are usually very feminine and wish to be admired for their looks, but hate themselves for their lack of will-power and compulsive vomiting.

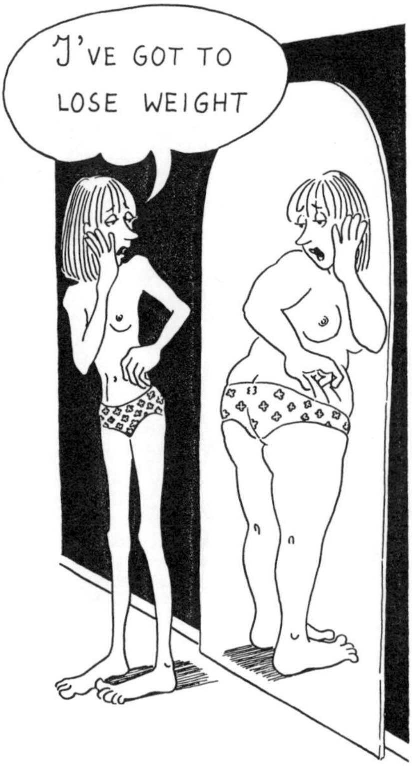

Anorexics and bulimics can be influenced by media images of supermodels, often being unaware of the fact that many fashion models chain-smoke or are on heroin or cocaine to kill their appetite, which keeps them slim and admired.[3] Besides, hard drugs overcome jet lag and give models sparkling eyes in front of the camera.

Bulimia and anorexia are widespread among girls who aim to copy or become supermodels, ballerinas or gymnasts.[4] Chemical imbalance in the brains of anorexics makes it impossible for them to accept how dangerously thin they have become. It is as though they are two people: an anorexic described how 'part of me looked in the mirror and said "Eat", while the other part said, "Help, I'm so fat, I *must* starve".' Anorexics and bulimics become anaemic, depleted of essential vitamins and minerals, moody and hell to live with. A few become clinically depressed, and in a small percentage of cases can attempt or commit suicide.

Professor Suzanne Abraham of Sydney University has successfully treated a large number of girls with eating disorders. She affirms that most of those who receive professional treatment will eventually recover. The treatment is lengthy and the patient *will* suffer from relapses. Only 5% of anorexics will die from complications or commit suicide.[5] Professor Abraham told the author of this chapter the surprising fact that bulimia was identified as a psychiatric syndrome only in 1980. The number of bulimics has soared, but it is difficult to provide exact statistics as bulimics hide their disorder, often for years. There are many more girls suffering from bulimia than anorexia. A recently published seven-year survey of eating patterns among young female students at the University of Western Australia noted a 'dramatic' rise in numbers of bulimics.[6]

When Princess Diana admitted that she suffered from bulimia, her widely-publicised confession gave self-induced vomiting as a method of weight control social respectability among certain young girls who admired the Princess. One such girl, heartbroken by the Princess's death, lamented in the June 1998 issue of *Cosmopolitan*, 'No one understands *why* I was so upset when Princess Diana died. To me she was not a Royal, she was a friend, the *only* other person I knew who suffered from bulimia.'

Princess Diana at the Taj Mahal
(Photograph P.A. News)

♥ A Real-life Story ♥

THE WORLD'S MOST FAMOUS BULIMIC

As a result of her parents' stormy marriage, their divorce and her motherless childhood, Diana, Princess of Wales, suffered psychologically. She had dreamed of being a ballet dancer but grew too tall to achieve her ambition. Instead she became the vulnerable, shy and blushing nursery-school teacher who thrilled the world when she became engaged to Prince Charles.

The Princess's bulimia was triggered by Prince Charles' comments that she was 'chubby' and by seeing herself on TV wearing a blue suit, which she feared made her look 'fat and dumpy'.[7] Worried about appearing on TV at her wedding ceremony and about her husband's fondness for Camilla Parker Bowles, she dieted, released tension by bingeing on ice cream, then agonised about putting on weight. Soon the Princess discovered she could gain comfort from eating but still lose weight if she managed to make herself vomit.[8] Using this method she lost kilos by the time of her wedding, where, in spite of her nervousness, she performed brilliantly.

Her main reading material since her schooldays had been romantic novels by author Barbara Cartland (whose daughter became the Princess's stepmother). Yearning for a great and passionate love, the Princess feared that hers for the Prince was not reciprocated, although initially Prince Charles *was* infatuated with her beauty, her sweet nature and her concern for others. But the stress of being in the glare of publicity left her, still an immature young girl, exhausted and nervy. Releasing tension through bingeing on food and vomiting helped her cope with pre-marriage nerves.

By the time of her honeymoon she was vomiting four times a day. Chefs on the royal yacht were amused when the Princess consumed 'endless bowls of ice-cream', and even asked for bowls of custard to eat in the royal cabin.[9] But always there was another camera to face, another photo opportunity: so she continued crash-dieting, interspersed with eating quantities of ice-cream, custard and chocolates, then vomiting them up in secret in her private bathroom.

Photographed in Scotland after the honeymoon, she looked skeletally thin. She even fainted when visiting the World Expo in Canada, having eaten nothing but a few biscuits for days beforehand. Her passion for gymnasiums and exercise and her devoted care for others less fortunate than herself were typical bulimic behaviour.

A Real-life Story

Under stress from having to make public appearances and from marriage problems, she binged on comfort foods and took 'slimming' pills containing herbal laxatives. Her bulimic behaviour and her resulting mood swings gradually worsened. When pregnant with Prince William, the Princess gave up personal appearances and stopped inducing vomiting, for the sake of her baby. As a result her depression and mood swings abated and her former sweet and charming personality returned. However, after the birth she suffered postnatal depression.

Like all bulimics, the Princess denied her vomiting behaviour, even to herself. For years she refused to confide in the family doctors or psychiatrists who treated various members of the Royal Family and so remained untreated.[10]

Bulimics present a sunny, feminine exterior, under which they conceal hurt, deny their problem and channel enormous effort into helping others. Princess Diana became loved and honoured worldwide for her work with sick children, lepers, battered wives and AIDS victims and for her role as loving mother. She kept hiding her eating disorder from the public. Her whole metabolism became deficient in potassium and essential vitamins, causing more fits of depression, mood swings and outbursts of jealousy, which worsened as her marriage crumbled and she became even more jealous of Camilla Parker Bowles.

Only after her divorce did the Princess, after struggling with bulimia for a decade, seek treatment, following the threat of public disclosure by a close friend, who feared she might kill herself. Finally the Princess consulted Dr Maurice Lipsedge, of Guy's Hospital, London, who made her acknowledge her problem and decrease her preoccupation with food and weight. She kept a diary of *everything* she ate. She was made to eat sensibly three times a day and release tension by methods other than binge-eating and vomiting.[11]

Dying so young, the much-loved Princess became the tragic media heroine of the latter part of the twentieth century, mourned by admirers all around the world. She had successfully hidden her bulimia from the public for many years, probably unaware that so many teenage girls and young women shared this eating disorder with her. After the Princess had revealed her bulimia in Andrew Morton's book (for which she provided Morton with taped information), hundreds of girls who adored her and tried to copy her glamour and style found comfort in the fact they shared the terrible scourge of bulimia with the glamorous, slim Princess.

HOW *you* CAN HELP

- Persuade your dieting daughter that not everyone can look like a supermodel or Barbie doll or should *want* to. Explain that many top fashion models and pop singers are desperately insecure in a competitive world where good looks rule. Such heroines are *very* flawed role models with a short shelf-life — why not find others?
- Explain that bodies starved of food start hoarding energy, which turns to fat once the dieter eats again.
- Mums should *not* complain about their weight or shape in front of daughters. In 1998, Joan Collins provoked a furore when she wrote in *The Spectator* that fashion is led by 'gay style gurus who must loathe women' and 'anorexic, androgynous teenagers who stalk the catwalks like heroin addicts in search of a fix'. Many fashion designers seek to change women's shapes to fit their own androgynous idea of female beauty. Forty years ago fashion models weighed 8% *less* than the average woman, now most supermodels weigh up to 23% *less* than the average woman. Pressures from the fashion world on girls to diet are enormous.
- Pin up photos of well-rounded girls rather than supermodels. Tell your daughter that few men like women who are all skin and bones. Explain how anorexics and bulimics have foul-smelling breath and can get stomach pains, anaemia and fits of depression. Does she really want to join them?
- Beware if she wails about being 'fat' or is frequently tired and moody. She may be smuggling food from the table in a napkin (or feeding it to the dog). See if she makes frequent visits to the bathroom or toilet after meals. Don't be fooled if she takes over the cooking and fusses round, offering food to everyone else. Anorexics frequently do this to cover up the fact that *they* are not eating.
- If she needs help, persuade your daughter to see your GP, who may treat her or refer her to a psychiatrist or specialist in eating disorders. The sufferer and her parents can also benefit by joining an Eating Disorders Support Group. If none is available locally, some doctors in country areas recommend attending meetings of Alcoholics Anonymous to deal with what is also an obsessive disorder, using the same techniques of group support.

TOBACCO: THE FACTS

THE GREATEST CAUSE OF DISEASE IN THE WORLD

In many countries tobacco companies, now seen as marketing death in return for dollars, are banned from advertising in magazines and on television, so they employ spin doctors to insert cigarettes into stage plays, films and magazine illustrations targeted at adolescents. The tobacco companies' hidden agenda is, 'Hey, kids! Smoking is sexy, sophisticated and cool!'

Only recently tobacco advertisements on billboards and TV have been banned in some countries. The World Health Organization claims that smoking is 'the greatest cause of disease in the entire developed world'. Cigarette and marijuana smoking are *major* causes of lung cancer and cancer of the mouth and tongue. Intent on staying slim, many girls choose to ignore the fact that smoking can cause an early death. If girls smoke and diet, and do *not* take added calcium in milk or calcium tablets, they may get bone fractures, due to premature osteoporosis. According to some physiotherapists and doctors, this is now occurring in relatively young women today.

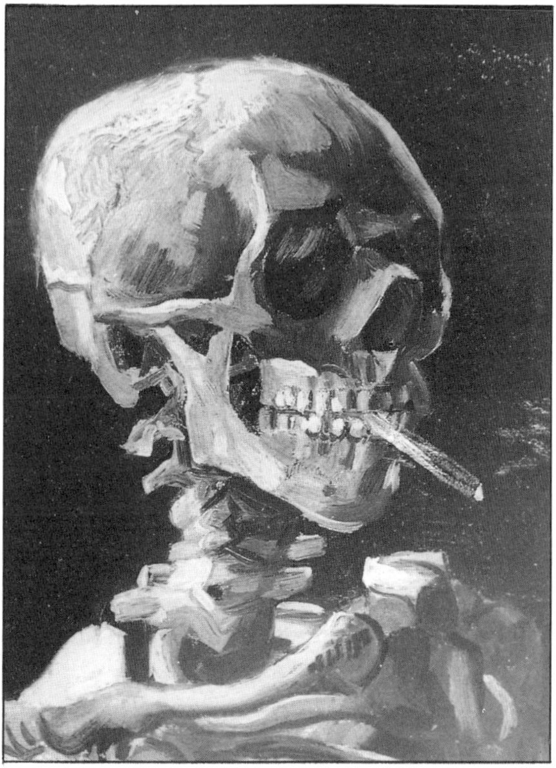

SKULL WITH CIGARETTE
Oil painting by Vincent van Gogh.
Rijksmuseum Vincent van Gogh, Amsterdam.

IMPORTANT POINTS

SMOKING IS A HEALTH HAZARD

- Nicotine in cigarettes stimulates the brain but three drops of pure nicotine can kill an adult. Smoking causes cancer and is a major cause of heart disease and infertility in women.
- Smokers have 15 times more chance of developing lung cancer, 8 times more chance of developing heart disease or a heart attack and are 10 times more likely to die from lung or tongue cancer than non-smokers. Smoking also contributes to osteoporosis.
- Deaths in men from lung cancer have dropped, but a higher smoking rate among women, many of whom use it to arrest appetite, has resulted in increased deaths in women. Tar is released from cigarettes in the form of particles in inhaled smoke. Black sticky tar collects in the lungs, causing cancer. Smoking 20 cigarettes a day over a year means inhaling half a cup of tar.
- Smoking is directly linked to gastric ulcers, chronic bronchitis and asthma. In women 73% of cancers can be directly linked to smoking. Some 34% of all female bladder cancers can be attributed to smoking; female smokers have a greater risk of developing cervical cancer.
- Passive smoking, or even being in the same room with a smoker, can injure the lungs of all those around the smoker. Smoke, inhaled from the burning end of a cigarette, contains more poisons than mainstream smoke. Passive smoking harms foetuses and babies in their cots and contributes to cot death (SIDS). In the face of so much adverse information, it seems incredibly stupid that girls are smoking at an earlier age and in larger numbers than boys.

WHY ARE RELATIVELY YOUNG GIRLS SMOKING?

Girls who take part-time jobs have enough disposable income to buy cigarettes and many believe smoking makes them look sophisticated and grown up. Pre-teen and teenage girls are highly influenced by their clique or peer group. If your daughter's clique smokes,

doubtless your daughter, keen to be popular and part of the 'in group', joins in. Everyone in the teen and pre-teen group wants to do exactly what the others do. Smoking often starts at a time when girls reject parents' values and rebel against authority. Smoking is legal and girls see adults doing it. Adults have heeded health warnings and are now smoking less. However, girls as young as ten or eleven are now smoking, finding it attractive because it reduces their appetites.

Pre-teens and teenagers are TWICE as likely to smoke if both parents smoke; FOUR TIMES as likely to smoke if parents and older siblings smoke.

It is far easier not to start smoking than to give up. Smoking is addictive. Some 80% of smokers want to quit when they read about the dangers but suffer from withdrawal symptoms when they stop or cut down their nicotine intake. They feel tense and nervous, develop headaches or eat more. Your daughter needs your support at this time.

IF YOUR DAUGHTER SMOKES THIS IS LIKELY TO HAPPEN TO HER

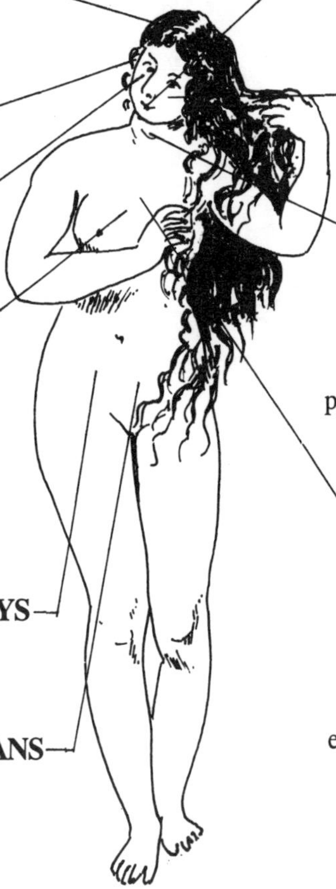

THE BRAIN
Speeds up, then slows down its activity. Dizziness (only in novice smokers).

EARS
Increased risk of hearing loss.

EYES
Watering and stinging.

HEART
Increases heart rate.
Raises blood pressure.
Greater risk of heart attacks and strokes.

BLADDER AND KIDNEYS
Increased risk of painful cancer.

REPRODUCTIVE ORGANS
High risk of infertility.
Less robust babies at birth.

BLOOD VESSELS
Become narrow, causing:
a. Premature ageing
b. Risk of gangrene
c. reduced blood supply to heart and brain.

MOUTH AND LARYNX
Risk of very painful cancer.
Staining of teeth.

TONGUE AND NOSE
Dulls sensation of taste and smell.

BRONCHIAL TUBES
The smoker becomes more susceptible to colds.
Reduces filtering action of the tiny hairs that stop dust particles from entering lungs.
Coughing.
Respiratory infections.
Chronic bronchitis.
High risk of cancer.

LUNGS
Shortness of breath.
Great risk of cancer.
Emphysema (loss of elasticity and deterioration of lung walls creates severe breathing difficulties).

NERVOUS SYSTEM
Tremor of hands.
Muscles tense up.

HOW *you* CAN HELP

ENCOURAGE YOUR DAUGHTER NOT TO START SMOKING OR TO QUIT

- **Don't smoke yourself and set a bad example**. If you can't stop, don't smoke in front of her and explain that it's how *you* releax.
- **Warn her not to start**. Nicotine contained in all cigarettes is a highly addictive as well as a deadly poison. At first, the nicotine stimulates smokers. Then, after a while, it relaxes them — producing the 'feel-good' effect. Years later it can kill them or render female smokers sterile for life. Is she prepared to risk being unable to have a baby later in life or having a baby which is less than robust?
- Tell her that *all* smokers have foul or 'ashtray' breath and their teeth will eventually be stained brown with tobacco. **Smokers look much older than they really are**, because their skin wrinkles faster and becomes dry and dingy. Smoking tobacco is definitely *not* something cool or sexy that makes women attractive. Those beautiful colour advertisements for cigarettes in magazines showing glamorous young people smoking and frolicking beside pure mountain streams are nothing but lies. The sad and unglamorous truth is that smokers are blackening their lungs with sticky tar. Many will die prematurely from cancer and other diseases or spend years and years coughing up phlegm.
- **If your daughter is earning good money** from a part-time job, encourage her to save for something worthwhile, or a holiday, rather than fritter the money she earns away on cigarettes.
- **If she has already started to smoke, set a firm date with her to quit**. Then, if she finds she cannot stop, encourage her to talk to former smokers, who will tell her how *they* managed to quit. If she finds she needs help, she should join an anti-smoking group or consult a psychiatrist or psychologist who specialises in this area. Her general practitioner can provide a prescription for slow-release **transdermal patches**, which contain a small dose of nicotine to help with initial withdrawal symptoms, like headaches, tension or disturbed sleeping patterns. Encourage her to persevere if she values her health and her complexion.

TEENAGE ALCOHOL ABUSE

DRINKING TO GET 'LEGLESS'

Parents are now facing severe problems caused by heavy alcohol consumption amongst some adolescents who sneak out of the house for Friday and Saturday night drinking binges. Addresses of some of these venues where teenagers drink to get blotto or pass out are now on the Internet. On university campuses, in all-male schools and colleges, male clubs and pubs, teenagers are drinking to 'get pissed' and as a means of 'having a good time'. They ignore the fact that large quantities of alcohol will, over the years, cause stomach ulcers, inflammation and decay of the liver (cirrhosis), liver cancer, heart disease and brain damage. Women, due to their lower body weight, develop these problems far sooner than men. Alcohol is also the *main* cause of road deaths in young people.

In the nineteenth and early twentieth century a large proportion of Australian men drank to get drunk, an attitude inherited from the nation's convict past. From 1788 onwards rum was illegal currency among convicts and the soldiers who policed our shores were known as the 'Rum Corps', because they sold (and drank) so much of the stuff. Drinking to get blind drunk was one of the few 'relaxations' available then, so one can understand why many Australians' attitude to alcohol is still bound up with the country's past. Due to the culture in which they've been raised, many Australian kids follow a similar pattern and think it's fun to drink to get blind drunk.

In contrast, most people from European wine-growing countries regard drinking wine with a meal as natural. They regard adolescents (or adults) who get drunk or vomit in their streets brutish and degrading. The author of this chapter used to live in Spain and each year attended the Fiesta of San Fermin in Pamplona. As a Spanish speaker, she was often asked by the Spanish police to translate and help bail out from the local jail good 'Aussie blokes', who were drunk as skunks on cheap 'vino tinto'. The Spanish police wondered why these tourists used their leisure time to drink in bars until intoxicated. For their part, the Bazza Mackenzie clones found it hard to understand just why the Spanish objected to behaviour which they found entirely normal and part of a good holiday.

During student initiation week on campus of some Australian universities, drunken boys and girls reel out of parties and collapse on the lawn, many vomiting. This sort of behaviour now occurs also on campuses across America and Europe. Where alcohol is permitted in colleges and fraternity houses, alcoholism and sexual harassment have become worse. Accusations of rape on campuses by drunken male students all over the world are increasing.

Concerned authorities who try to help schoolchildren to become aware of dangers of alcohol, claim that alcohol is by far our biggest drug problem today. In some tough inner city secondary schools, nearly a quarter of Year 7 and Year 8 students binge-drink (a binge being defined as over five standard drinks a session) each weekend and some drink till they drop.[1]

The new pre-teen game is 'Pissed in the Park' and unfortunately it's a game that girls as young as nine or ten are playing.[2] A volunteer youth worker with Drug-ARM in Sydney told us that some of these girls have run away from home and are living on the streets or in squats. Others sneak out from home at night, once parents are asleep, and drink in the park with older girls and boys. DrugARM do their best to help these young people under extremely difficult circumstances.

MORE TEENAGE GIRLS DRINK TO EXCESS THAN BOYS

Boys don't want to ruin their chances of sex by getting 'brewer's droop' from drinking too much. When trying to 'score' with a girl, they slow down consumption and concentrate their efforts on giving alcohol to *her*, fully aware that once girls are drunk, they will offer little resistance to having unprotected sex.

The Salvation Army sees a lot of pre-teenage girls drunk in city streets. Major Brian Watters of the Salvos Rehabilitation Service recently revealed that when he started working with alcoholics twenty years ago, the vast majority of their clients were 'skid-row' men in late middle-age. Now it's quite common for the Salvos to have alcohol-addicted kids of twelve, thirteen and fourteen for treatment.

Of course, not all adolescents drink. But when they do, many lack reasonable restraint. Most girls become intoxicated faster than boys as they have less body weight: a few glasses render them easy prey to predators and then they may well submit to unprotected sex.

WHY PRE-TEEN AND TEENAGE GIRLS BINGE-DRINK

DrugARM, an organisation that deals with teenage drug problems, operates throughout Australia and New Zealand. DrugARM's New South Wales director believes low self-esteem and a desire for peer group status are behind most teenage drinking. 'Kids out there believe they are immortal,' he says sadly. 'They fail at school, feel worthless, so they look for something that will give them notoriety and status in their group. If they can't get a good reputation, a bad reputation's better than nothing, far better than being ignored at school or at home.[3] Kids are clever at getting what they want. They steal alcohol from parents or buy it from bottle shops and pubs that don't care *whom* they sell it to.'

Some kids ask their parents for money for school lunches; they save up and then get someone of legal age to buy them a carton of beer or spirits. Under-aged children with money can easily buy alcohol from supermarkets that stock Asian rice wine for cooking. Another supermarket favourite with kids is a cooking wine called 'The Cook's Friend'. Both wines contain 17% alcohol and can be bought legally by children from supermarkets. No one queries their age when they go through the checkout with a bottle of cooking wine. Some kids get hold of their parents' credit cards or buy or find stolen ones, ring the bottle shop and order crates of beer or spirits to be delivered to the cardholder's address at a specific time. Then they wait outside, tip the driver and sign for it, telling the driver that the crates or bottles have been ordered by their father.

Under-aged children who earn money from part-time or full-time jobs can pay cash. They ring up bottle shops, give the name of a householder and wait till the delivery van arrives. Satisfied by a cash payment, the delivery man hands over crates of beer and spirits, then drives away. The kids gleefully cart the crates round to the nearest park and the party begins.

Today, some girls as young as fifteen, often earning money from boring and menial part-time jobs, go out in groups to get what they call 'pissed' or 'to have a good time'. Each Saturday night in our cities and country towns, young girls attend parties where they drink quantities of spirits and full-strength beer, but rarely drink wine or low-alcohol beer. Some take bottles to parks, city streets or beaches, mingle with other weekend drinkers and get 'legless'. When blind drunk, they are at risk from vandals and hoons, sexual predators, casual unprotected sex and, of course, those sexual dangers, Hepatitis B and AIDS.

Eighteen percent of girls under seventeen now have five or more alcoholic drinks a week. These drinks are not five glasses of table wine, consumed with food around the table at home in a leisurely fashion on five different nights. No way. All five drinks are imbibed on the same night (usually a Saturday) during an all-night 'rave' or a party in a deserted park or sports oval.[4]

A major problem for young female drinkers is how to get home after an evening's drinking. Some lurch drunkenly across the road and cause traffic accidents. Those injured by cars are carted off by ambulance and end up in hospital or in the morgue. Others get into cars driven by someone over the legal limit and are involved in a crash.

Parents should be aware that statistics show that road accidents in which alcohol consumption is involved are now the major cause of death in young people.

HOW *you* CAN HELP

- Your daughter should regard alcohol as something to enjoy, but only with food. When she turns twelve, let her have a glass of wine (or wine and water as French children do) with a meal **on special occasions**, provided she sips and savours it slowly, rather than gulps it. Usually, children who are allowed to sip ***one*** glass of wine a night under supervision encounter far fewer problems with alcohol than those banned from 'the demon drink', who may then start to drink illegally.
- Impress on her just how stupid and unsophisticated it is to drink alcohol when food is not provided to act as 'blotting paper'.
- Explain how drinking spirits or wine, glass after glass, releases inhibitions and can be a crucial factor in unsafe sex. Alcohol takes effect on the brain within *ten minutes*. Due to lower body weight, most women have a *far* lower tolerance to alcohol than most men. Alcoholism causes liver cancer, heart disease and brain damage, all developed by women sooner than by men.
- Tell your daughter *never* to enter a car when the driver is under the influence of alcohol or drive herself when over the limit. Give her a phonecard to call home if you cannot collect her from parties. A cabcharge card could save her life as young partygoers often have little idea of potential dangers after a party.
- If you discover that your daughter has been binge-drinking, ask her the following questions:
  - Are you drinking because you have a problem to blot out or simply 'to have a good time'?
  - In a group situation, where booze is being passed around, do you feel *calmer* when the bottle reaches you?
  - Do you hang on to the bottle *longer* than your friends do?
  - Are you suffering from *short-term* memory loss? For example can you remember what you *wore* last Saturday?
- If you are worried about your daughter's fondness for alcohol, call your local Alcohol and Drug Information Service for advice, inform your family doctor and/or join Alcoholics Anonymous.[5]

ILLEGAL DRUGS

THE FESTERING SORE OF MODERN SOCIETY

Taking or smoking illegal drugs (as well as some legal drugs such as alcohol and tobacco) are seen by many teenagers as an acceptable way to block out problems in our Prozac-taking society. Many kids think that recreational drug-taking is a good way to enjoy themselves. It is tragic that such a warped message has influenced young people. The *real* facts about illegal drugs are:

- **There can be absolutely *no* shortcut to long-lasting happiness by taking or smoking mood-altering drugs: it doesn't *solve* anything. They simply make everyday problems *worse*.**
- **Drugs undermine people's physical and mental health, their ambitions and power of thought.**
- **The effect of drugs wears off quickly so that greater quantities have to be taken to banish 'midweek blues' after a weekend's pill-popping or injecting.**
- **Most drugs affect the user's driving skills and coordination, vision and ability to judge distance and speed. Anyone under the influence of drugs or alcohol who kills or injures another person while driving can be sentenced to prison. Drugs can be detected by testing blood and urine samples.**

Some teenagers refuse to read drug warning pamphlets; others 'switch off' during school drug education programs. Drugs are now freely available to the young, often given out as free samples by schoolgirl or schoolboy pushers. Parents *must* read up about drugs and remain one step ahead so they can talk with their children while their kids are still young enough to heed warnings.

MARIJUANA – THE SLOW BRAIN DRAIN... AND WORSE

Marijuana, pot, cannabis, dope, grass or weed are all names for the dried leaves and the flowers of the hemp plant. Which country has the highest per capita consumption of marijuana? India? Jamaica? The answer is Australia, followed by Holland, where its use was decriminalised decades ago. The Dutch sell it in milk bars and cafes and masses of teenagers smoke it openly. Illegal consumption in the USA, in Britain, most of Europe and New Zealand is considerable.

A recent survey indicated that almost *half* the population of Australia aged between 14-34 have tried cannabis. It grows well in Australia backyards, so it is widely available in many schools and at parties. Ready-rolled 'reefers', 'tokes' or 'cones' can be bartered for doing another kid's homework. School kids buy a 'reefer' and inhale the smoke, curious to know how marijuana will affect them and keen to be part of the 'in crowd' that uses it. The majority who experiment with pot do *not* become regular users, but some will.

Passing around 'cones' means saliva is passed on as well, with the consequence that smokers with ulcers or tiny cuts in their mouth can catch hepatitis. Some who smoke pot inhale amyl nitrate or 'rush' at the same time to achieve a bigger 'high'.

A small minority 'snow cone' (adding cocaine to their 'cone'). Relative to pot cocaine is expensive, so its use is low among the young. Apart from 'snow coning' cocaine can be snorted or injected, like heroin, making the user feel confident and relaxed.

WHAT MAKES TODAY'S MARIJUANA MORE TOXIC?

Cannabis is the equivalent of Prozac for today's teenagers and far more widely available. The chemical in cannabis which gives users a 'high' is THC (Delta-9 tetrahydrocannabinol). THC affects the mood as well as perceptions of the user. It reduces will-power and taken over a period causes short-term memory loss. Hashish is a much stronger form, manufactured by compressing marijuana resins into small blocks.[1] It can be mixed with tobacco and then smoked. 'Hash is extremely potent. Those who have used hash discover that the THC level in it is so highly concentrated that even a small amount will produce a 'high'. Hash marinaded in butter or hash oil can be put into a cake mix, baked and served as 'hash cakes' or biscuits.

This mind-altering drug contains 421 known chemicals, some of which remain stored in body fat and in the brain for up to one month before being excreted from the body. Some of these chemicals and the tar content of marijuana are just as harmful to lungs when inhaled, even in small quantities, as those in tobacco. The real problem (which some people choose to ignore) stems from the fact that users of marijuana are now smoking 'improved' or hybrid strains, like sensimilla, which contain at least 15% THC. These strains are far stronger than the ones hippies smoked way back in the 1960s, when marijuana contained only 3% of THC. In the 1960s pot smokers would have needed a 'joint' as long as an axe handle to inhale the same quantity of THC as present in one single 'joint' today! Harmful effects of heavy pot smoking are loss of short-term memory and concentration, lack of all will-power and motivation, detachment from reality and anxiety. Loss of concentration is what makes it hard for heavy marijuana smokers to achieve good marks at school or university, or hold down a responsible job.[2] Pushers don't explain that what they are selling as 'high quality' pot, guaranteed to give a really *big* 'high', may be 'cut' with cocaine or heroin. This can lead to addiction of the buyer (and profit for dealers), which, of course, greedy, unscrupulous pushers won't tell.

When fathers boast to kids, 'I used to smoke pot all the time when I was at university and I managed to get a good job and a nice house,' the fathers are talking about far milder form of marijuana than most kids smoke today.

Many girls experiment with pot — some will decide they don't like it, others smoke a few 'cones' but will eventually give up. A third and smaller group will smoke heavily — some will have unprotected sex when 'high' and may get pregnant. Unfortunately for pot smokers, home-rolled 'cones' lack filter tips and 'bongs' (plastic water bottles with hose attached) do *not* filter out tar. Hardened pot smokers inhale deeply and delay exhaling which can eventually cause lung cancer, because sticky tar builds up in their lungs.

A Real-life Story

HOW POT CAN LEAD TO HARD DRUGS

From the smog of Germany's industrial Ruhr, we came to subtropical Queensland in search of a better life in an unpolluted land. My Dad migrated to Australia with Mum, my brother, my twin sisters and me. Dad's long-term goal in migrating was that his four children would grow up in the warm climate of Queensland where we could attend university — he worked long hours to achieve this.

Unknown to my parents, my brother Paul and my twin sisters were introduced to marijuana by one of their school friends. Together they grew their own pot on a former Council rubbish tip, where it flourished undetected amongst the weeds. They always had a good supply to smoke themselves and to sell to others. For years Mum and Dad never suspected that three of their children grew and smoked pot. I was the only one not involved. As the eldest daughter I had become more responsible than the younger kids. I went to university, fell in love with a fellow student, married him and had two children.

My twin sisters, four years my junior, were high-spirited and very attractive. Unlike me, they were not at all ambitious. Smoking pot with my brother and his friends gave them thrills, but little motivation to study or stay on at school. They decided to drop out after Year 10. Both of them refused Dad's offer to pay for further study. Mum became deeply involved with New Age philosophies, horoscopes and numerology, which Dad found exasperating. Their marriage foundered, they drifted even further apart and divorced.

It was a great shock to my father when Paul and two of his friends were arrested and convicted of dealing in marijuana. Mum insisted Paul had been 'victimised': his friends were guilty, not him.

My twin sisters had a series of dead-end jobs and a string of boyfriends — nothing lasted long. One boyfriend introduced the twins to LSD, crack and heroin. Soon they needed large sums of money to satisfy their drug habits. Then, one of the twins was arrested for housebreaking and went to jail. That was the turning point: finally, I was able to persuade both my sisters to enter a methadone program.

Now, years later, my twin sisters share a rented house and are still on methadone. They look many years older than I do — their teeth are rotting, their gums bleed. They have no jobs, no money; they are lonely and embittered, but unfortunately there is little I can do for them now. Mum, locked in her own dream world as a New Age guru, still refuses to believe that Paul still sells drugs and grows marijuana somewhere hidden in the bush.

AMPHETAMINES, LSD AND KETAMINE

Amphetamine or 'speed' can be snorted in powder form, injected (being at risk from HIV or Hepatitis B when needles are shared) or drunk with liquid. Speed causes a 'high' by raising blood pressure and by increasing the heart rate. It is illegally sold as an appetite suppressant. Speed and LSD trips (which look like small pieces of blotting paper) make users feel alert, confident and energetic, but at high doses users can become paranoid and, after some hours, many vomit. (Should this happen in your home, make the child in question clear up the mess, your sympathy will *not* help them.)

LSD interferes with the brain's ability to store experiences. The brain's cortex becomes overloaded with sensory input, which forms the basis of psychedelic experiences, visions where colours split and explode and a mundane object like a chair seems to promise infinity. Cheaper than Ecstasy, LSD, in large quantities, has unpredictable side-effects and used with marijuana can be dangerous. LSD users have been known to jump out of ten-storey buildings, laughing as they went. All over the world, ageing patients with LSD-induced schizophrenia are frittering away their lives in psychiatric wards or halfway houses, thanks to this drug.

Ketamine, known by kids as Special K, an animal anaesthetic, with hallucinogenic properties similar to LSD, is now a popular party drug. In high doses ketamine can cause users to lose consciousness. Girls have been raped under its influence.

THE AGONY OF ECSTASY

Ecstasy tablets and powder were developed in Germany before World War I for use as an appetite suppressant. In 1965 a group of Californian psychiatrists started using it to release patients' inhibitions, combining Ecstasy with LSD with disastrous effects on some patients. As a result it was banned.

Ecstasy, known as 'E' or the 'hug drug', was exported illegally from America, then resold in Britain and Australia for $120 to $140 a tablet. When the formula to manufacture this complex drug became available on the Internet, illegal laboratories sprang up in many developed countries. To make it more affordable, illegal labs 'cut' their tablets with cheap fillers such as talcum powder or polluted heroin. Before prices dropped to $40-$60 a tablet, some dealers sold fake 'E' tablets, which were only inexpensive dog-worming tablets or those large white toxic tablets obtainable from aquarium shops to control gill fluke and lice in fish tanks. Fish cleaning tablets cost only a few dollars each, give users a buzz, then make them vomit. Some pushers make a packet out of selling these to credulous teenagers, before decamping to fresh fields. One way of refusing 'E' without seeming a wimp is to query if it's worth spending $60 on fish-tank cleaner or a dog-worm pill as 'E' tablets do *not* carry the maker's address or any guarantee.

Tablets can be white, cream, pink, yellow or green. Some have brown flecks, depending on what type of filler has been used to bulk them out. 'Ekkies', 'E' or 'White Doves' and speed keep users awake, so they can dance all night. Unfortunately, 'highs' have a down side, being followed by bouts of depression. Like speed (amphetamine) and LSD trips, 'E' is widely available at raves. These all-night parties are held in nightclubs, abandoned warehouses or empty dwellings, mainly at weekends, advertised in record stores and on the Internet. All over the world thousands and thousands of teenagers put themselves into a trance-like state after popping pills or powders. Many drink alcohol or take tranquillisers afterwards to help with the inevitable bouts of irritability, muscle pains, 'midweek blues,' that follow. Those who take designer drugs regularly may have difficulty with study or any form of work, except the most menial tasks.

Liquid 'E', GBH (Grievous Bodily Harm) or Fantasy is a clear liquid, sold in small glass bottles. Mixed with alcohol it can put experimenting teenagers into intensive care wards on respirators. Parents should be aware that teenagers often mix a cocktail of designer drugs, alcohol and tranquillisers, trying to avoid the depression that follows drug taking; 'midweek blues' play havoc with school or university study. Taking a cocktail of drugs (multi-drug use) makes users vomit and can cause 'road rage', violence or bouts of paranoia. Although such behaviour shocks many adults, to 'using' teenagers it's 'no big deal'. Users become hooked on 'highs' and return to raves each weekend for a further dose of their preferred hallucinogenic.

Drug dealers are no longer swarthy men in grubby raincoats hanging about outside the school playground. These days, avaricious schoolgirls and boys in expensive clothes and joggers sell 'party' drugs to kids like your daughter. If caught and arrested, a smart lawyer will plead for them in court, 'These children didn't know what they were doing'. There is now so much money in selling 'recreational' drugs to kids that pyramid-marketing chains extend down from illegal laboratories, through adult middlemen to teenagers. Schoolgirls and boys buy in bulk from the middlemen and resell 'E' tablets, speed, in powder and tablet form and LSD in schools and at all-night parties. These kids become so wealthy, they can afford to buy 'king hits' (ten doses) of recreational drugs, which they resell at a good profit to fund their own drug habit. This is the real reason why recreational or mind-altering designer drugs are widely available in many schools and at *all* social levels across America, Australia, New Zealand and Western Europe.

In 1995 a British teenager named Leah Betts, intent on 'having fun' at her eighteenth birthday party, took three Ecstasy tablets. Carried away by Ecstasy and the deafening thump of the music, Leah, the life and soul of the party, danced on in a frenzy, blissfully unaware that her body temperature and blood pressure were rising. She drank a great deal of water to make up for the dehydrating effects of the drug. Her overloaded system was unable to eliminate enough fluid through sweating or urination, which affected her brain. Finally, Leah collapsed and died.

Ecstasy is now taken by *all* social classes in many different countries. Deborah Hanger, teenage daughter of an affluent, well-connected Brisbane barrister and an eminent child psychiatrist took three Ecstasy tablets, determined to dance the night away. Before dawn she, too, was dead. After her death, some of her friends from an exclusive girls' private school Deborah had attended, horrified their parents by admitting they *also* had been offered Ecstasy tablets by a fellow pupil. None admitted to taking 'E' but confirmed just how *easy* it was for them to sample it.

Thirteen Australian girls have now died from taking Ecstasy. Compared with the long-term harm from smoking tobacco or the many road accidents involving teenagers under the influence of alcohol, the death rate from Ecstasy is *not* high, considering its wide use among adolescents today. However, taking 'E' *is* rather like playing Russian roulette — it comes from illegal laboratories, without *any* form of guarantee, none of the buyers can tell *which* tablets are lethal and which are not.

A Real-life Story

ECSTASY AND ANNA WOOD

Anna Wood was outgoing, popular and part of an affectionate group of friends, who adored her. Her parents were united, stable and loving. Anna had everything to live for. She was pretty, bubbly in personality, had a happy home life and was about to leave school and take her 'dream job' as a beautician.

Like many fifteen-year-olds, Anna was keen to attend a Saturday night 'rave' in the city but, fearing her parents would forbid it, she told a 'white' lie. She reassured her parents she was only going to watch videos at her friend Chloe's house and 'sleep over' there.

According to Angela Wood, Anna's mother (who allowed us to print Anna's photograph in this book in the hope that her story may prevent other teenage deaths), Anna looked just as she does in her photograph on the fatal evening when she went to a 'rave' party. Unknown to her parents, Anna and her group of friends aimed to take Ecstasy and 'have a good time'.

Each girl paid $60 for an 'E' tablet. Anna bought her lethal tablet from Samantha X, a Year 12 student at Anna's high school. Samantha had been 'dealing' for some time and stood outside the entrance to the all-night 'rave' selling Ecstasy. Anna had been against heroin and other hard drugs but had occasionally smoked marijuana and had once taken half an Ecstasy tablet. Some of her friends had experimented with a range of drugs, although Anna had told them they were stupid to do so. On this particular occasion, Anna bought and swallowed with water a whole 'E' tablet, worried that taking half, like her friends, might not give her 'a good trip'. Anna danced for hours, saying, 'This *is* the best night of my life.'

She became very thirsty. As Anna didn't want to drink alcohol, she drank masses of water. She danced on... and on... and on.

At 5 o'clock in the morning, Anna started vomiting. Rave-goers are used to this, as it happens a great deal to kids on Ecstasy or a cocktail of drugs. However, Anna's vomiting continued for so long that her friends became alarmed. By now her eyes were rolling wildly and she had no idea where she was. Her friends dragged her into a car and drove to her friend Chloe's home, where Anna continued vomiting and lost consciousness.[3]

Anna's mother, Angela Wood, was called. She summoned an ambulance which sped her to the Royal North Shore Hospital. Terrified of the police, Anna's friends lied to cover up the fact that they had all taken 'E'.

A Real-life Story

They told the ambulance man that Anna's drink had been 'spiked'. Finally, at the hospital, Anna's terrified friends confessed they had *all* taken Ecstasy. By now it was too late. Doctors ordered a cerebral angiogram, which showed that Anna's brain had swollen with all the water she had drunk, so no blood or oxygen could reach it. She was brain dead.

Anna's friends and family were confused, angry and distraught by her death. They demanded to know how a fellow pupil at Anna's school could sell a trusting young girl with her whole life ahead of her a tablet that would kill her.

The police took the matter very seriously. Samantha, the schoolgirl from Sydney's northern beaches who sold Anna the fatal 'E' tablet, was arrested, tried and found guilty. Samantha and her family employed a top Sydney barrister, who made emotional pleas about her youth as an extenuating factor and she got off relatively lightly, with a good behaviour bond and community service.[4]

Angela Wood has converted her grief and anger over her daughter's death into a crusade to save other teenagers. An attractive woman and an excellent speaker, Angela visits schools and parent groups, lecturing on the dangers of drug abuse. 'I see speaking in public as the gift Anna left me, to save other kids from what happened to her,' Angela says.

WHAT CAN HAPPEN WHEN A BOY OFFERS A GIRL 'E'

More often than not, boys with the necessary $40-$60 buy an 'E' tablet in order to offer it to unsuspecting girls. This is one reason why more girls than boys consume Ecstasy and more girls than boys have died from it. Not that 'scare' stories seem to stop girls from trying it or amphetamines, which they often combine with smoking to lose weight. When a teenage Romeo offers Ecstasy tablets to your daughter, he explains that these magic pills will enable her to dance all night without getting tired. However, he has a hidden agenda.

Romeo, like his mates, believes Ecstasy has a more powerful aphrodisiac effect than amphetamines or marijuana and that he is bound to 'score' if he can only persuade Juliet to swallow an 'E' tablet. It takes twenty minutes for 'E' to enter the bloodstream and be carried to the brain where it increases the circulation of a substance called serotonin. This chemical, which occurs naturally in the brain, triggers feelings of confidence, affection and excitement. Boys believe it will get girls in the right mood for sex, although Ecstasy is not actually an aphrodisiac and has variable results.

In some girls, provided the tablet has not been cut with LSD or worse, Ecstasy can give an adrenalin-like rush then relax the user and, where romantic music is played, create a situation of intimacy, ideal for a girl to feel that she is attracted to a boy and falling in love. At first, Romeo and Juliet dance vigorously. Then, as soon as he sees Juliet look relaxed and mellow, Romeo requests slow music and they dance cheek-to-cheek, their bodies entwined. After a suitable interval he pressures her to have sex with him. If she refuses, he will try to convince her that everyone else is having sex, so why not her? If she hesitates, he may well demand, 'Why not? Are you frigid or lesbian?'

Faced with mounting pressure from Romeo, and under the sensuous influence of Ecstasy, Juliet eventually yields and has sex for the first time. She is totally unprepared. She never wanted to be seen by her friends as 'cheap' by carrying condoms around with her and she is not on the pill. Romeo thinks condoms spoil his pleasure so never carries them. Under the influence of Ecstasy, Juliet has unprotected sex with a boy she hardly knows, risks getting pregnant and catching HIV or Hepatitis B.

HOW TRACEY BECAME ADDICTED TO 'E'

A Real-life Story

Tracey, a sixteen-year-old hairdressing apprentice from Parramatta, was invited by a girlfriend to an all-night rave in an empty house in one of Sydney's wealthy eastern suburbs. She didn't know a soul there except the girlfriend who had invited her, who had told her that dress was casual. Surrounded by 'cool' boys and girls from Sydney's top private schools, Tracey felt ill at ease and out of her league. They all seemed to be enjoying themselves, smiling and laughing a great deal. In the meantime Tracey's girlfriend had disappeared.

A tall, attractive, blond-haired boy approached Tracey and introduced himself as Simon. 'Want to dance all night?' he asked. Bowled over by his good looks, Tracey agreed. Simon led her to the bathroom, where he produced three white tablets and offered her one. Tracey didn't want him to think she was an unsophisticated 'Westie', and to look 'cool' accepted a pill without question. Simon offered her a glass of orange juice to accompany the pill as Tracey didn't drink alcohol. Within an hour the Ecstasy took effect, Tracey's shyness vanished, she felt happy, talking and laughing a lot. Now, they all seemed lovely, beautiful people. Strongly attracted to Simon, she danced close to him all night without getting tired.

After the rave, Simon persuaded her to have sex in the back of his car. From then on, Tracey has been going to raves with Simon each week, dancing and getting high on 'E'. She worries that Simon has never taken her home to meet his mother in spite of all her hints.

Tracey now takes the pill, terrified of getting pregnant. Ecstasy has given her memory loss and bad attacks of the 'midweek blues'. Previously she enjoyed talking to clients in the hairdressers but is now silent and morose at work. She no longer goes to evening classes as part of her job training. Sometimes she wakes up feeling so ill that she phones in sick. Tracey is not aware that her boss is considering firing her. Her widowed mother is worried, but Tracey clams up and won't talk to her, afraid her mother will find out she is on the pill.

Half the time Simon's divorced parents have no idea where he is and don't care. His father doesn't see him often but gives him an allowance large enough for him to buy Ecstasy in bulk and resell it to friends. Tracey can't feel happy without getting high on Ecstasy and being with Simon, although she knows that he is not serious about her. The chills and feelings of despair she experiences during the week are getting worse. Now she needs three times as much 'E' to 'feel good'. Without knowing it, she has become addicted.

HOW *you* CAN HELP

INFORM YOUR DAUGHTER ABOUT DRUGS

- The time to talk with your daughter about drugs is *before* she and her friends start using them. Under the age of ten, most kids still listen to *your* beliefs and *your* advice. This is when you should warn her about their bad long-term effects.
- Warn your toddler not to taste *anything* she finds in ampoules or packets either on the streets or in parks. Explain that it could be a substance that could harm her or make her sick.
- Explain the difference between 'good' medical drugs and bad or illegal drugs when she is six or seven. If your daughter gets sick and is prescribed a 'good' drug, use this as an opportunity to explain how important it is not to overuse medication or turn to 'bad' drugs when she is older.
- Between 9-11, your daughter will slowly start to move away from your influence. If, at this age, she hasn't been informed about the dangers of drugs by you, she will hear about them from friends or through the mass media, possibly in a distorted way.
- Don't leave drug education entirely to her school. Talk with your teenager about what drug education she is getting. Do not give her a lecture. A car or a shopping expedition can be a good place for a quiet chat. Ask nonchalantly how many girls in her class smoke pot or take recreational drugs. Her answer could surprise you. Remember, many 'nice', intelligent kids now buy and experiment with a cocktail of drugs, some with fatal results.
- Should you find what you think is pot or a bong (plastic bottle with a piece of hose attached) in your daughter's room, you should not blame yourself for bad parenting. Many 'good' parents are struggling with their children's drug abuse today. Making an angry scene doesn't help. Don't *stop* parenting at this point. Ask if she takes drugs to have 'fun' or to escape from reality. Recommend counselling and go with her initially. If possible, she shouldn't come home to an empty house. Be there for her, even if she doesn't want to talk about drugs or any other problem. Be consistent and remember, teenagers *need* an adult authority figure to react *against,* which should be you!

- Although tripping on LSD provides beautiful floating feelings, it can also give 'bad trips' and under its influence people have killed themselves in car accidents or suicided. LSD (and/or contaminated heroin) is often added to 'E' tablets, LSD being far cheaper to manufacture than Ecstasy. Warn your daughter against getting into a car with *anyone* who has taken drugs of any kind as that person's judgment will be seriously impaired.
- Parents need *all* the information they can get to help teenagers resist sales pressure from the kids who now push drugs in many schools. Some kids offer trial 'hits' for free. Discuss with your daughter exactly why they do this: is it because they like her, or do they do it to build up their sales and make more money?
- If your daughter comes home from a party 'high' on drugs, *don't* try to discuss *anything* until the next day. Stay calm; anger won't help you or her. Look in your phone book, contact your local Community Drug and Alcohol Service (you don't need to give your name) or other voluntary anti-drug organisations who are discreet and experienced. If in doubt, ask your family doctor to recommend one and find the counsellor whose approach suits *you*. Don't give her a large allowance which could be a temptation to buy more drugs. *Always* check up with other children's parents if your daughter asks to stay overnight with a friend.
- Join a parents' group run by an anti-drugs organisation with whom *you* feel in sympathy. Today all cities have many such organisations. At this difficult time you and your partner need support and practical help. Group support works well for parents driven to despair, trying to live with an adolescent on drugs which causes trauma in everyone's lives.
- If your daughter brings drugs home, you have the right to insist that *your* house remains drug free and/or call the police if you fear younger siblings may start taking drugs. If under 17 she will have to appear in a juvenile court (except in Tasmania) and be cautioned or fined. Some parents refuse to pay the fines and insist on the offender working to pay them off. Each case is different and each family reacts differently. By now you may need a social worker, counsellor or psychiatrist specialising in this area to provide help. Detox is used only for heroin and cocaine rather than for designer drugs: it can work only in cases where the drug taker is *truly* motivated to change her life.

- **No one on 'E' should drink alcohol or take more than 500 mL of water while dancing or 250 mL while sitting down. Alcohol, if combined with Ecstasy, liquid 'E', Ketamine or Fantasy, can cause kidney or brain failure**.

  Teenagers who go to raves regularly should make sure they can recognise symptoms of drug overdose, such as nausea and vomiting, fainting on the dance floor, inability to urinate, overheating or convulsions.

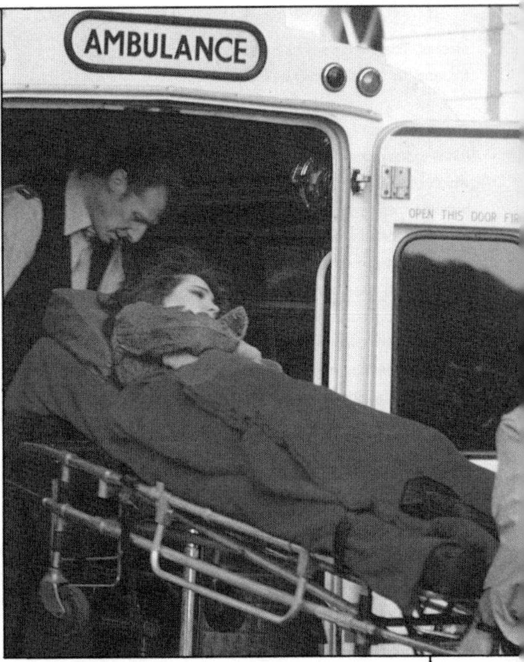

- If your daughter attends raves tell her that if someone who has taken 'E' vomits or faints an ambulance *must* be called. Meanwhile, someone should fan the sufferer to keep her body temperature down. When the ambulance arrives, the driver must be told exactly what the person has taken. She mustn't cover up. Doctors *need* to know what drugs have been taken to treat a drug patient successfully.
- If teenagers throw a party in your house, make certain you stay home, however unpopular you are with your kids. Say firmly to any young guest who smokes pot, 'You are welcome to do whatever you like in your *own* home. But as a guest in my house, please respect *my* way of life.' Parents have rights as well as children. Insist gatecrashers leave immediately. Gatecrashers could bring with them 'spiked' alcohol or illegal drugs, with dire consequences for you and your children.

VIOLENCE AGAINST YOUR DAUGHTER

That your child might suffer the pain and humiliation of childhood sexual abuse or of rape or sexual assault as a teenager seems unthinkable. But it happens often enough that parents should think about how to respond if it happens to *their* daughter.

CHILDHOOD SEXUAL ASSAULT AND INCEST

The World Health Organization estimates that between 36% and 62% of all victims of sexual violence are fifteen years old or younger; Australian studies suggest rates between 20% and 28%. In spite of media hype about wicked strangers and organised paedophilia, most perpetrators are known to the child and are very often in a relationship of trust — father, stepfather, grandfather, uncle or long-time family friend. This dreadful betrayal of trust adds a great psychological burden to the harm inflicted on the child.

It is, of course, a betrayal of the mother's trust, too. It may be very hard to believe that this can happen, because it involves not only accepting that your daughter has been violated and hurt, but that someone you love and trust has done this. Yet her capacity to cope will be affected by your ability to acknowledge what has happened and to respond to it.

Other things can also confuse a mother's reaction. There is a general unwillingness to face the facts of incest and sexual abuse in our society and sometimes attempts are made to downplay it, even to blame the young victim. A few years ago a Canadian judge reduced the sentence of a child molester on the grounds that the three-year-old female victim was 'sexually aggressive'. Some people, even some in responsible professional positions, think children make this sort of thing up. Perhaps a few do, but fantasy like this could indicate that something is wrong somewhere; a wise parent would consider what this might be, rather than ignore it.

Children expect that adults, especially those close to them, will protect them from pain and harm. When, instead, they inflict this upon a child, she is betrayed, confused and may feel somehow guilty and responsible. It can be hard to trust anyone afterwards.

This makes it very difficult to tell another loved authority figure, even a mother, about the abuse, particularly as the child is usually sworn to secrecy. She may feel 'dirty' and ashamed and think she has somehow forfeited the right to receive help. She will realise that her mother will find it incredible that someone she knows, a friend or relation, could do this. Very few children disclose sexual abuse. Therefore, if your daughter has enough courage and faith in you to tell you, directly or indirectly, that she has been subjected to unwanted sexual activity, she deserves your wholehearted support.

You and your daughter may both need help to come to terms with the situation: medical or psychological attention, advice about what to do next and how to minimise possible long-term effects. Contact your doctor or one of the specialised organisations listed in the front of the telephone directory. They will not be shocked — sadly, they will have heard many stories like yours before. Childhood sexual abuse is most commonly inflicted on girls by men, so your daughter may be more comfortable if the people you ask to help her are women, particularly when it comes to any physical examination.

Although childhood sexual abuse is a criminal offence, the processes of bringing the perpetrator to justice can be long and very painful. It can be hard to get a conviction, and if the victim knows the offender walked out of the court unconvicted, this would be the final betrayal and sign that she is of little value in our society. You might think that taking the matter to the law would do more harm than good. Talk it over with someone you trust, bearing in mind that there are matters which professionals working with children may, by law, have to report to the police.

What happened to your daughter and the blow to her self-esteem and ability to trust others may lead to a number of problems, ranging from poor concentration at school and isolation from friends to high-risk behaviour during the turbulent teenage years and difficulties in personal and sexual relationships as an adult.

It may be a good idea to talk to her teacher, so together you can work out ways to ensure her education doesn't suffer. Love, reassurance and acceptance at home will be of fundamental importance. Obviously, protection from situations where she could be vulnerable to further abuse is essential.

High-risk behaviour can include smoking, drinking or bingeing alcohol or using illegal drugs. It may take the form of sleeping around or not using contraceptives and condoms to protect against pregnancy and sexually transmitted infections. Studies show that a high proportion of young teenage mothers have suffered childhood sexual abuse. The reasons for this are complex, but low self-esteem and feeling that sex is the way to approval are likely to be factors.

Pregnancy and labour can be more difficult for women of any age who have been victims of violence. These women often face more health problems than other mothers and their babies are likely to weigh less at birth, which can mean more health risks for them.

No matter how old your daughter is when she becomes pregnant, intimate physical examinations and labour can trigger or revive memories of the past abuse. This can cause reactions which neither she nor her midwife or doctor understand and can affect the care she receives. Suggest that things will be better for her and the baby if she tells her main carer about the abuse. At this time she may be more comfortable being looked after by women rather than by male doctors or nurses.

RAPE AND SEXUAL ASSAULT

What can you do if the unthinkable happens and your daughter is raped or sexually assaulted? Rape crisis centres now exist in all big cities and there are also free anonymous telephone crisis lines. Look them up (they are usually listed in the front of the telephone directory) and suggest to your daughter that you or she contact a centre or call a phone service. Emergency services offer help and counselling or refer you to other services if necessary. They are staffed by specially trained women who usually have a very woman-centred outlook on the world.

These specialised services are not just for help at the time of the incident. Your daughter could find them useful even if the rape or assault happened a while ago. Remind her about these services as time passes in case she changes her mind or needs more support as she works through what has happened.

Get appropriate medical help. The Accident and Emergency departments of most hospitals have guidelines to make sure victims of violence are seen quickly and treated sensitively. You may prefer to go to your general practitioner, especially if she has a good rapport with your daughter. Rape or sexual assault may or may not involve physical injury. Research suggests that it can also cause long-term health problems. As well as making sure your daughter gets medical attention in relation to possible injury, infections or pregnancy, you need to know of the chance of long-term effects on her health.

Always respect her decisions. What happened to her took away her dignity and autonomy, her control over her body and most intimate aspects of her life. This feeling of powerlessness could have a more lasting impact on her than any physical injuries. It is very important not to reinforce it by making decisions for her or by overlooking her opinions and feelings about what should happen next. This may be very difficult in an acute crisis, but at least make sure she understands that you are trying to support and help her until she can take control again herself.

This is no time for recriminations. Bite back any criticism which may come to you in your anger, denial or distress. Remember, *no* girl *ever* deserves to be raped or sexually assaulted. Victims are never responsible for the violence inflicted upon them — no one has any right or excuse to treat another person in a way which degrades and hurts her like this.

Recognise that the violation of your daughter can be a trauma, though of a different kind for you. Don't be afraid to ask for help for yourself. You will be able to support your daughter better if you are coping better yourself.

Report the matter to the police if your daughter agrees to this. Obviously, you should contact the police as soon as possible if you want to lay criminal charges. Your daughter should understand that she will have to undergo physical examination and answer a lot of questions which would be unpleasant and embarrassing at the best of times. She will probably have to tell several people what has happened, in a way repeating and reliving the event.

These days there are more women among the doctors who do the forensic examinations. And, like the police who deal with cases of sexual violence, they usually have special training to enable them to satisfy all the legal requirements as sensitively as possible. You, or someone else your daughter would like to support her, can be with her. The rape crisis centres can usually provide an experienced woman to do this if she would be more comfortable that way.

Most victims don't report rape, unless it was inflicted by a stranger or they were physically injured. Charges are not always brought against the perpetrator if they do. Many find the idea of going through the experience again in front of a court just too much. Again, the decision must be your daughter's, with calm advice from you and other members of the family and maybe your own doctor or lawyer if you have one. Obviously, this advice must look to your daughter's best interests and long-term healing, though it may sometimes be hard to overcome gut reactions for vengeance.

HOW *you* CAN HELP

IF YOUR DAUGHTER IS SEXUALLY ASSAULTED

- **Listen to your daughter**. Recognise that you may instinctively want to deny what she is trying to tell you or to avoid dealing with it. Remember, it is even harder for her to tell you about it than it is for you to hear about it.
- **Believe your daughter** when she has the trust and courage to tell you what happened. If you deny her this acknowledgment, you reinforce her sense of betrayal and alienation.
- **Trust her**. Don't recriminate or put your feelings or family interests before hers. She is your daughter and has a right to your support and protection.
- **Encourage and support her to regain control**. As a victim of sexual assault she has had her autonomy and control over her body torn from her. She needs you to help her make decisions about what to do next, not to make them for her.
- **Seek professional help** with her consultation and agreement
- **Make sure she knows you love her, accept her and support her** in this crisis and whatever may follow. Reassure her often that the victim is *not* the guilty party and that while she may feel ashamed about what happened, she was not to blame.

DOMESTIC VIOLENCE

If you are in a situation of domestic violence, your children are likely to be harmed by it. This may be through physical injury, though the psychological and emotional impact of living in a violent household can have an effect as profound as actual physical violence. Children are almost always aware of violence in their home and very often experience it themselves. Inevitably, their own distress is made worse by knowing about their mother's suffering.

It is easy for outsiders to give glib advice about leaving a violent relationship and taking children to a safer environment. Only you can decide what you can or should do. Investigate your options. There are specialised services to help women in this situation in all big cities. They include anonymous telephone services, information and referral centres, refuges and safe places where you and your children can stay until you decide what to do next.[1]

Think long and hard about the accepted wisdom that a stable home with their own father is best for children, no matter what it is like. You can discuss this with your daughter if she is old enough, bearing in mind that, like you, she is probably confused and ambivalent, torn between her love for her father and the horror and fear of what he sometimes does. She may blame you, or herself. She needs to know that violence is *never* justified, never an acceptable response, no matter what provokes it.

The decision to leave a violent relationship is a very difficult one, unless you or the children are obviously at great immediate risk. If you decide to reject your situation as unsafe for you and your children, discuss your choice with your daughter. If you don't, she may misunderstand and blame you for separating her from her father. The role of the single parent is not easy, but you will cope better if both of you understand why this seemed the best option.

It is not uncommon for children to feel somehow responsible for the violence inflicted on their mother. They are *not*, and every effort should be made to let them know this.

You and your children must remember that those who behave violently toward others are responsible for their actions. No one else is.

DANGEROUS SEX

According to general practitioner Dr Jean Sparling, there is evidence to show that those girls who receive the most information are the *least* likely to develop dangerous sexual habits. Dr Sparling is known by her patients as an excellent communicator. She explains the importance of getting your pubescent daughter to come to terms with the danger of sexually transmitted infections, which can seriously affect her health and jeopardise her future.

NORMAL VAGINAL HEALTH

The healthy vagina contains moisture in the form of mucus coming from the gland in the neck of the womb (cervix); these glands manufacture a small amount of clear vaginal discharge with a characteristic 'female' smell, which will normally leave a yellow colour on the underpants. The vagina always contains organisms, bacteria, fungi and viruses, which are a normal part of the contents and form a well-functioning and healthy ecosystem. The normal vagina does *not* need cleaning with douches, creams or perfumed sprays. Contrary to the advertising for them, these will only upset Nature's perfectly balanced system. If your daughter has any vaginal discharge in excess of the normal, any itching or offensive odour whatsoever, she should see a doctor.

The infections described on the following pages are roughly in order of frequency rather than their danger to health and well-being.

CHLAMYDIA

(Pronounced klamideeyear). A very common disease: 50,000 new infections occur each year in Australia (23% occur among secondary students in the 13-18 age group)[1]. Chlamydia normally has an incubation period of 1-2 weeks, but may be slightly longer. Often the infection causes no obvious symptoms. When there are symptoms, these consist of a vaginal discharge (watery *or* sticky), itching and pain on passing urine. The most likely person to suffer from chlamydia infection is a sexually active female under 25, who is in a monogamous relationship and whose partner is not using condoms. The disease often occurs when the girl changes partners. The main complication of the disease is the spread to the pelvic area with an infection in the womb and fallopian tubes (the tubes through which the eggs from the ovaries travel to enter into the womb) which, in many cases, can lead to infertility.

Diagnosis is usually made from laboratory testing of urine or from a swab taken, possibly when having a pap smear. Urine samples are more reliable as they do not need the organism to be kept alive for testing.

Treatment. One oral dose of azithromycin will eradicate this organism. It is important to trace all sexual contacts the girl may have had, going back for several months if possible.

CANDIDIASIS OR THRUSH

This is a fungal infection and may or may not be an STD (STI).[2] It *can* be acquired through sexual contact or in a wide variety of *other* ways, including taking broad-spectrum antibiotics (an unwelcome side-effect of which may be the killing of 'good' protective vaginal flora, thus causing candida to flourish), wearing tight nylon pants or sitting around for long periods in a damp bathing suit. Candida is often found in chronic invalids or following a debilitating illness.

Candida presents as a very itchy, white, cheesy vaginal discharge without an odour. It causes intense discomfort. It often mimics the feeling of sexual arousal, but then makes sexual intercourse disagreeable or even painful for the female partner, though not for the male.

Treatment is by one of several antifungal agents (applied by vaginal applicator). Tablets are also given by mouth, as the candida may have lodged in the bowel. It is important that the girl's partner is also treated with antifungals, because he may well have been infected with candida. Even though the male appears to have no symptoms, he may still be able to pass candida on (or 'ping-pong' the candida back again) by having sex with a girl who is undergoing antifungal treatment.[3]

GENITAL HERPES

The herpes simplex virus infects most people as cold sores, eye infections or genital herpes at some time in their lives. Genital or herpes simplex virus type II, previously thought to spell disaster to any young woman's sex life, no longer needs to be thought of in this way. The incubation period varies from 3-6 days. At first the infected area feels hypersensitive; this is soon followed by a group of small painful ulcers on the labia, clitoris or inside the vagina. There may be similar lesions in the mouth and throat following oral sex. These symptoms may persist for up to three weeks. In those who have not previously met the virus in any form, initial infection may be extremely painful and debilitating (rendering vaginal sex out of the question both from the aspect of pain and from the danger of infecting a partner). A swab taken from the ulcer is the most effective way of making a diagnosis.

Treatment is with antiviral agents such as aciclovir and valaciclovir. It is most important to treat the initial illness promptly and properly. Improperly treated genital herpes is a relapsing condition, occurring over many years, that has profound sexual and social consequences. It is important to realise that this condition may be transmitted even when no ulcers are visible. Cure is seldom achieved. Repeated courses or continuous treatment may be required to keep the patient symptom-free. Relapse may be associated with physical or emotional stress, fever, menstruation and many other conditions affecting well-being.

GENITAL WARTS

Human papilloma virus (HPV), also known as venereal or genital warts, is usually sexually acquired. These warts, sometimes but not always painful, usually occur around the openings to the vagina or bowel. Lesions may occur up to six months after infection. The wart virus can be a cause of cancer of the neck of the womb. Warts may be small and flat on cool dry areas or large and feathery on the moist areas. Warts on the neck of the womb often have no symptoms. As they are not visible, they remain undetected and are usually found coincidentally when a lab is checking on the patient's pap smear. Many different types of wart virus have been identified. Some viruses have a low risk of cervical cancer, while others are associated with a markedly higher risk. Factors such as smoking, numbers of sexual partners, lowered immunity and the presence of other sexually transmissible infections also influence the development of HPV-induced cervical cancer.

Treatment of external warts is by local application of Podophyllotoxin paint. This is best done either by your doctor or a family member. It is not recommended that girls treat themselves. If this treatment is not successful or the warts are internal, other methods, such as cryotherapy and laser treatment, are available through your doctor. Patients with genital warts must be checked for other STDs. In view of the risk of cancer it is most important to have regular follow-up pap smear tests. There is a high recurrence rate, even after treatment. HPV vaccines are currently being developed and future patient management may well be by this means.

HUMAN IMMUNODEFICIENCY SYNDROME (HIV-AIDS)

Acquired Immunodeficiency Syndrome (AIDS) follows infection with human immunodeficiency virus (HIV), acquired through exchange of infected semen, saliva or blood.

Clinically, this is an acute illness with fever, night sweats, malaise and acute discomfort, headache, general aches and pains and a generalised rash which occurs about six weeks after the initial infection. Chronic lethargy and depression may persist long after the acute phase of the illness has passed. Blood tests usually become positive within the first three months following infection. After this most people enter a phase where they are symptom-free, which lasts for a period ranging from several months to many years. However, HIV-AIDS is a complex disease and can have many variations. During 1997 there were major advances in our knowledge of HIV infection. There are now follow-up tests to assess the progress of this disease and several new drugs are now available to slow its progress.

Treatment currently consists of a combination of drugs, which have been found to work much better than any one drug used alone. The lone drug is disadvantaged by the ease with which the virus can develop resistance to it. Combination therapy reduces this factor. The aim of treatment is to keep the patient as well as possible for as long as possible. At present there is no known cure for this fatal disease, although some people remain well for prolonged periods.

HEPATITIS B

This is a serious virus infection, causing permanent damage to the liver and, in some cases, *death*. It is transmitted in exactly the same ways as AIDS but is even more infectious. There is no really effective treatment once the disease is caught. Fortunately, there is now a vaccine to prevent it and this vaccine is being offered to all children in Australia and New Zealand, along with their other 'shots'. Vaccination is to be given to eleven- and twelve-year-olds with two injections, one month apart, and a booster dose after six months. Side-effects are minimal and vaccination is strongly advised.

TRICHOMONIASIS

(Pronounced trick-oh-moan-eye-aysis). This is a common cause of vaginal infection. Sexual intercourse is the principal means of transmission. The incubation period varies from four days to four weeks after sexual contact. It presents as a vaginal discharge which is offensive, frothy, yellow-green and purulent. Some patients also have an intense vulval itch or tenderness, making intercourse unpleasant. Others have no symptoms at all from this disease. Diagnosis is made in the laboratory from a vaginal swab of the discharge taken by the doctor.

Treatment is by specific antibiotics taken by mouth. Sexual partner(s) should be notified by the sufferer.

GONORRHOEA

(Pronounced gonner-rear). It has an incubation period of 2-7 days but may vary from 24 hours to a month. Infection with this organism in teenage girls is high (20% according to the La Trobe Faculty of Health Sciences study). The disease often goes unnoticed because there may be no symptoms at all. If symptoms do occur, these can include vaginal discharge, frequency of urination, painful intercourse, malaise, aching, fever, abdominal and joint pain. Some women have a heavy, yellowish vaginal discharge accompanied by irritation. The infection may ascend to the upper pelvis and result in infection of the womb and fallopian tubes, resulting in permanent infertility. Diagnosis is made by a swab taken from the vagina.

Treatment is by antibiotics and usually effects a cure.

SYPHILIS

Previously thought to be well under control, syphilis is now on the increase again in certain parts of the world and in certain ethnic communities. Incubation is about 21 days after contact. The first manifestation is the 'chancre', a firm, painless, punched-out ulcer on the vulva or inside it. If this chancre goes unnoticed, it will get better on its own. The glands in the groin are usually enlarged, firm but not painful. Untreated, the disease persists in the body for as long as 20 years in some cases, ending in insanity and eventual death. If the chancre is detected (and this is rare), material taken from the base of the lesion may reveal the organism. Blood tests are also helpful.

Treatment is by antibiotics and, unlike the grim days of World War I when syphilis swept through the population and killed many, it is now curable.

SCABIES

This is a form of dermatitis which is not usually regarded as an STD but can be acquired by sleeping with someone with scabies or being in close contact for a prolonged period. Following infestation by the mite (*Sarcoptes scabiei)*, a month or so later nocturnal itching and a rash will appear on hands, wrists, forearms, waist, inner thighs, buttocks and ankles. The mites which burrow into the skin can be seen under magnification.

Treatment is by application of paints or creams such as benzyl benzoate or lindane 1% cream. Bed linen and clothing should be treated.

IMPORTANT POINTS

- It is important to teach your daughter from an early age to wipe herself **from front to back** after defecating or urinating. This method *must* be used in order to avoid dragging germs from the bowel across the vaginal and urethral entrance.
- She should be encouraged to use loose-fitting cotton underwear. After swimming girls should change out of damp bathing costumes into dry ones *immediately*.
- Your daughter should *always* insist on 'no condom, no sex' as the pill provides no protection whatsoever against STDs. Due to the dangers of oral infection with Hepatitis B and AIDS oral condoms are now available.
- Accurate information about bodily changes, STDs, vaginal infections and the good and bad points of condoms are essential to help your daughter understand **the vital importance of safe sex practices**. Teach her to respect her own body. If you provide answers to her questions from an early age, there is no embarrassment because to her this is 'just another part of learning' and has no different connotation from learning how to cross the road. This is the time to communicate *your own* sexual and family values. Show her what loyalty, trust and other values, important to you, mean and how they work. **Example works far better than 'preaching'**.
- Give her the facts while she is still young enough to listen, rather than in the phase when she will not wish to be questioned by an anxious parent and will go to great lengths to avoid this. Explain **before puberty** to your daughter that the emphasis on safety for women has now changed from the need to avoid pregnancy to the very real dangers of STDs. Explain that safe sex includes measures **she must take** in order to prevent unwanted pregnancy, minimise the chances of contracting a sexually transmitted infection and avoid the violence associated with sexual activity, prevalent today.
- One myth popular with teenagers is that the contraceptive pill provides them with protection from STDs — in reality it **only lessens the risk of pregnancy**. It has absolutely **no effect** on lessening the dangers of diseases acquired by sexual means. Many infections can now be transmitted through sexual activity. Some are insignificant; others can be deadly. You and your daughter must learn about them, so that she can be alerted to the dangers, avoid them if possible, and, if not, at least be aware of warning signs.

IN CONCLUSION
THE BOND OF PARENTHOOD

Contributors to this book have achieved successful careers and, between them, have raised two dozen children. The message that they impart is that girls must be taught to think clearly and positively, to make *logical* choices, to have a sense of values and self-esteem and a vision of what they can achieve in life.

The section on parents' nightmares was distressing to compile. However, in a world, where casual sex, drug-taking, alcoholism and rape are viewed on TV as well as in life, today's parents *must* be well-informed in order to guide and protect their daughters.

Not only mothers feel pain as teenage daughters grow away from them — fathers often experience pain and loss on seeing another man receive the adoration formerly reserved for them. Take heart! Once the turbulence of adolescence is over, the closeness you previously experienced with your daughter should return. For those experiencing problems with teenagers, remember, although the bond that links you may appear tenuous or fractured in adolescence, it still remains. Whatever you do, keep a dialogue going — let your daughter know that your door is always open. Meet, write or telephone as often as you can. The mother-daughter bond will strengthen again when your daughter finally settles down and raises her own children. Then she will realise just how much you did for her when she depended on you. She will groan, 'Did *you* go through all this too, Mum? It's so hard!'

The wheel of life turns inexorably. Eventually, your parents will die, bringing you face to face with your own mortality. Then, as you age, your daughter will worry about you and you may depend on her for things you once could do easily yourself. During old age, it is often a great comfort for parents to live close to daughters, who, if they are lucky, will shop for them, drive them to doctors and care for them when they are sick. The bond of love that you forged with your daughter in her childhood is a deep-seated one that should last a lifetime.

DEDICATION

In fond memory of a close friend and outstanding writer, Professor Derek Llewellyn-Jones, who shared with us his love of literature and art as well as his ready wit and his medical knowledge. Derek Llewellyn-Jones broke new ground as the first medical specialist to write highly readable paperback books on women's health aimed at the general public. His research in the field of women's health and his best-selling books, *Everywoman* and *Everygirl* (written with his wife, Professor Suzanne Abraham) have been inspiring to other writers on female health. The Derek Llewellyn-Jones Memorial Foundation has been established at the University of Sydney, New South Wales. All donations to this Foundation will be used for research into women's health.

ACKNOWLEDGMENTS

Thanks to Jill Richardson for photographs of her daughter Lucy and for her advice; to those members of the de Vries family who appear in some photographs; to Adri Smit for her delightful line illustrations; to Jake de Vries for book design; to Liz Hatton and other teachers who kindly shared their expertise with us; to Professor Suzanne Abraham of Sydney University who generously shared her knowledge and expertise in dealing with eating disorders; to Jan McGuffog and others who provided real-life stories and to Marusia Maccormick for research and photographs.

We also thank Dr Cherrell Hirst, OAM, Chancellor of Queensland's University of Technology and Director of the Wesley Hospital Breast Cancer Clinic, for launching *Raising Girls*.

Thanks to Catherine Hammond Editing Service, Sydney; to John Simms Proofreading Service, Brisbane; to literary agent Selwa Anthony; to Australian distributors Michael Rakusin and the staff at Tower Books and to Paul Parkinson and staff at David Bateman Publishers and Distributors of Auckland, New Zealand. Last but not least, thanks to Jacqui Gallagher of Jacq Productions, Sydney, for publicity and advice on cover lay-out and to our printers Prestige Litho, Brisbane, for their care in the printing of this book.

PANDANUS PRESS, Brisbane, Australia.

ENDNOTES

THE TENDER AGE

1 The following baby and childcare books will provide detailed assistance:
Green, Dr C. *Babies!* Simon and Schuster, London and Sydney, 1992
Green, Dr C. *Toddler Taming*. Doubleday, Sydney and London, 1998.
Davies, Ann. *Confident Parenting*. Souvenir Press, London, 1997.
Leach, Penelope. *Baby and Child*. Penguin, Melbourne, 1998.
Gressor, Megan (editor). *Raising Kids: A Parents' Survival Guide*. Gore & Osment Publications Pty Ltd, Sydney, 1997.

2 For help with breastfeeding, in Australia contact your local branch of the Nursing Mothers Assocation or the La Leche League in New Zealand.

3 Henderson-Smart, D.J., Ponsonby, A.L. and Murphy, E. *Reducing the risk of sudden infant death syndrome*. Australian Journal of Paediatrics and Child Health (1998), pp. 213-219.

BECOMING A PERSON

1 Community Child Care Co-operative Ltd (NSW) have issued excellent guidelines and a childcare check list, which is available free of charge.

2 Kramer, Rita. *In Defence of the Family*. Basic Books, New York, 1983. p.100.

THE LEARNING PROCESS

1 Irvine, Dr John. *Who'd be a Parent?* Pan MacMillan, 1998.

2 Marris, Michael. *Teenagers: A Parent's Guide for the 90s*. Millennium Books, Sydney, 1997. Written by a New Zealand psychiatrist.

3 Marris, Michael. *Op. cit.*, p. 92.

BECOMING SEXUALLY MATURE

1 Susanna de Vries. Views expressed in her book *Strength of Purpose, Australian Women of Achievement, 1900-1950*. HarperCollins, Sydney, 1998.

2 Moderate to severe acne responds to cyproterone, taken for 21 days each month; it can reduce acne after four months' treatment. Benzyl peroxide, tetracycline or erythromycin are also used. In severe cases isotretinoin, derived from retinoic acid, can be used but can react badly with sunlight.

3 *Girlfriend* for March 1998 contained a sexually explicit article called *Do the Tongue Tango: Become the World's Best Pash Princess.*

4 Lindsay, J., Smith, A. and Rosenthal, D. *Secondary Students. HIV/AIDS and Sexual Health, 1997.* Centre for the Study of Sexually Transmissible Diseases, Faculty of Health Sciences, La Trobe University, Melbourne, 1997.

5 Kostash, Myra. *No Kidding: Inside the World of Teenage Girls*. McLelland & Stewart, Toronto, 1987, contains documented case histories of many schoolgirls having sex but bored by it after a time and doing it only 'to keep their boyfriends happy'.

6 From interviews with Susanna de Vries (see also endnote 1 of this chapter).

7 See footnote 4. Material cited by Lindsay, Smith & Rosenthal.

BULLYING AND STEALING

1 Study published March 1998, Rigby, Dr Ken, University of South Australia, and Slee, Dr Phillip, Flinders University, South Australia, and Rigby, Ken, *Bullying in Schools.* ACER, Hawthorn, Victoria, 1993.

2 Many teenage suicides in Australia (the country with the fourth highest rate of teen suicides in the world) have implicated bullying at school coupled with severe family problems at home.

COPING WITH DIVORCE AND DEATH

1 1997 study involving Brett Behrens, Psychology Dept., University of Queensland; Margaret Anderson and Professor G. Williams, Social and Preventive Medicine; Dr Bill Bor, Enoggera Child and Youth Mental Service; and Dr M. O'Callaghan, Mater Hospital.

GOING SOLO – SINGLE PARENTHOOD

1 Figures provided by the Australian Bureau of Statistics and the New Zealand Government Statistical Service.

2 See also Burns, A., Macquarie University, and Scott, C., University of Western Sydney. *Mother-Headed Families and Why They Have Increased,* Sydney, 1994.

3 See 1997 University of Queensland interdisciplinary study between the Psychology Department, Social and Preventive Medicine, Enoggera Child and Youth Service and Mater Children's Hospital in which children of mothers who change partners frequently have higher rates of behavioural problems than children in stable single- or two-parent families.

4 Barrett, Maureen. 'Single Mothers Suffer more Ulcers', *Medical Observer*, 28 October, 1994.

5 In *Child Abuse and Neglect in Australia 1995-96,* Dept. of Child Health & Welfare, Canberra, A. Broadbent and R. Bentley report very high rates for child abuse and neglect. (91,734 notifications, over 39,000 of which, on investigation were substantiated. Among the proven cases, 51% of cases of abuse and severe neglect were among young single-parent families, In 1994 Millward, C. and Funder, Dr K. compared the problems of 153 sole and 1,226 double-parent families and found a high rate of dissatisfaction and/or depression among isolated single mothers living below the poverty line.

6 Kupke, Diana, *Me and the Kids. How to Survive and Succeed as a Sole-supporting Parent,* Penguin Books, Ringwood, 1987, discusses various ways for the mother to deflect anger against the child. So many single supporting mothers are having severe problems with older children that, to help them, Life-Line and some other charities and churches are providing a free counselling service, employing trained social workers and psychologists. The Life-Line service is free.

SURVIVING THE BLENDED FAMILY

1 Bloomsbury Press, London, 1988.

2 A blended family is 'a family with more than one child where at least one of these children is not the biological child of one or both partners in that family'.

3 The figures cited apply to Australia. The rates of failed second marriages in New Zealand, parts of Europe, Canada and the USA are also high.

ADOPTED CHILDREN AND THE DONOR DILEMMA

1 ABC TV. *Compass*. March 1998. A TV program on adoption, hosted by Geraldine Doogue in which all those on the program, except journalist Bettina Arndt (a widow who had raised a child as a sole parent), were against adoption. In Queensland the waiting time to adopt an Australian child can be 10 years or longer; in other States it ranges from 5 to 10 years.

2 ABS statistics reveal that in each year almost 35,000 fully investigated cases of child abuse and neglect take place among single-parent families in Australia. See Broadbent, Anne. *Child Abuse and Neglect, Australia 1995-96.* Child Welfare and Health Series, Canberra. Report 53 of the Australian Institute of Criminology, *Children as Victims of Homicide* by Heather Strang relates the poverty and instability among which these abused children are reared, how 'their mothers were often very younger and living in uncertain relationships'.

3 Cited as a news item in *Courier-Mail,* Brisbane and by Arndt, Bettina, in the *Sydney Morning Herald,* 9 May, 1998.

4 Search Institute of America. *Growing Up Adopted,* 1994. A study using a *randomly* selected group of 700 adopted children found above average rates for social adjustment, scholastic ability and family stability among adopted children. A very high proportion of these children were found to feel and be stable and much loved and have an overwhelming desire to succeed in life.

5 Eccleston, Roy. Dear Dad (whoever you are...) *The Australian Weekend Magazine*. Sydney, 18-19 April, 1998, describes the donor problem.

IF YOUR DAUGHTER IS A LESBIAN

1 Statement by staff member at Melbourne's Sexually Transmitted Disease Centre.

SCHOOLGIRL PREGNANCY

1 1996 census reports (ABS) show a 21% increase in single motherhood over the 1992 census. *The Australian*, 21 April, 1998.

2 Lindsay, J., Smith, A. & Rosenthal, D. *Secondary Students: HIV/Aids and Sexual Health, 1997.* Centre for the Study of Sexually Transmissible Diseases. La Trobe University, Melbourne, 1997.

3 Interview with author Susanna de Vries, Brisbane, 1998.

4 The State of Western Australia took steps to remove abortion from the Criminal Code in 1998 after attempts were made to prosecute two doctors who had provided abortions. Later that year the abortion laws were passed by the West Australian Parliament, making it the first State in Australia to legalise abortion.

5 Arndt, Bettina. *Sydney Morning Herald.* May 9, 1996 14-year-old pregnant Catherine Evans was told by a Queensland social worker that her child would eventually hate her if relinquished for adoption and was given the misleading impression that the Government would give her 'heaps of money and support'.

Against the wishes of her mother, who feared they could not afford to raise the baby properly, Catherine kept her baby.

EATING DISORDERS

1 Figure from a study presented at the 1998 conference of the Australian College of Paediatrics, reported in *The Weekend Australian,* 16 May, 1998.

2 Treatment for obesity is detailed in Abraham, Suzanne and Llewellyn-Jones, Derek. *Eating Disorders.* Oxford University Press, Sydney and Auckland, 1998.

3 Writer, L., 'Heroin, Models, Drugs and Weight-Obsessed Young Models'. *Who Magazine.* May 11, 1998. Cites former British model Kate Hatch revealing the amount of heroin abuse among models. Richard Maberley, Director of London's Select Models Agency, says that 'for models with an eating disorder heroin is like Christmas, *because on heroin they feel no need to eat*'.

4 Abraham and Llewellyn-Jones. *Eating Disorders* (see endnote 2 of this chapter). Cites the number of bulimics greatly exceeding that of anorexics. Various clinics state a figure is hard to obtain as many bulimics hide their problem for years and refuse to tell friends or family or seek professional help.

5 Cited by Associate Professor Suzanne Abraham of Sydney University in an interview with the author Susanna de Vries, in May 1998.

6 Seven-year study of first-year students by Mary Batik, clinical psychologist, Eating Disorders Clinic, Princess Margaret Hospital, Perth, 1998.

7 Account contained in *Diana, Her True Story in Her Own Words,* as told to Andrew Morton. O'Mara Books, London, 1997.

8 Morton, Andrew. *Diana, Her True Story in Her Own Words.* p. 56.

9 Morton, Andrew. *Diana, Her True Story in Her Own Words.* pp. 127-131.

10 Susanna de Vries' ex-husband worked for a time for Professor Sir Martin Roth, then Head of the Department of Psychological Medicine at the University of Newcastle and former President of London's Royal College of Psychiatrists, who at this period was consulted regularly by members of the Royal Family. Had the Princess revealed her symptoms Sir Martin would have been able to arrange treatment with a specialist in eating disorders. Ashamed of her self-induced vomiting, the Princess did not tell any doctors for a decade.

11 Princess Diana was, according to Andrew Morton's book, also helped by Suzy Orbach, author of *Fat is a Feminist Issue* and by a Sydney herbalist.

TEENAGE ALCOHOL ABUSE

1 Terry Metherell, Director of Life Education, Australia, 1997. Interviewed in 1998 by *The Bulletin.*

2 A 1997 report by NDARC on adolescents stated alcohol was the most commonly used legal drug and marijuana the most commonly used illegal drug. Rates of cocaine and heroin use among teenagers are much lower.

3 In October 1997, DrugArm's vans operating around Sydney helped 1,105 teenagers in trouble, most of whom were drunk. Due to soaring problems with children, they are placing an anti-drug and alcohol program on the Internet.

4 Revealed by an Australian survey in 1997.

5 Alcoholics Anonymous (AA) offer support to teenage alcoholics and their families through group meetings. For support for children with drug problems consult Narcotics Anonymous, DrugArm and Life-Line. Tough-Love support groups operate in cities in Britain, New Zealand and Australia and help parents with drug-addicted children and other behavioral problems. Centa-care provides Roman Catholic-based counselling services while Life-Line is non-sectarian and provides a free counselling service for parents in many towns in Australia and deals with a wide range of behavioural problems in children and employs trained social workers and psychologists. Due to widespread problems with children, there is now a wide choice of specialist counselling services for parents. What is important is to find one that suits *you,* your personality and beliefs. Additional names are listed under Drug and Alcohol Counselling in the Australian Yellow Pages. To find specialised parents' support groups in New Zealand contact your local branch of the Mental Health Foundation. The Community Alcohol and Drug Service (09-623-2323) are recommended by the New Zealand Mental Health Foundation for those with problems in this area.

ILLEGAL DRUGS

1. Informative pamphlets published by the Centre for Education and Information on Drugs and Alcohol (New South Wales Health Department). See also the book by Paula Goodyear, *Kids and Drugs.* Allen and Unwin, Sydney, 1998.

2 Trevor Grice and Tom Scott. *The Great Brain Robbery.* Allen and Unwin, Melbourne 1997, and Publishing Trust, Wellington, 1996.

3 Details of Anna's death provided by Anna's mother, Angela Wood.

4 Samantha X's full name was reported in the Sydney papers at her trial.

VIOLENCE AGAINST YOUR DAUGHTER

1 The World Bank estimates that, worldwide, domestic violence causes more deaths and incapacity among those of reproductive age than cancer, traffic accidents and diseases such as malaria. It is the leading cause of injury to women.

DANGEROUS SEX

1 Lindsay, J., Smith, A. and Rosenthal, D. *Secondary Students: HIV-AIDS and Sexual Health.* Faculty of Health Sciences, La Trobe University, Melbourne, 1997. p. 11.

2 STDs (sexually transmitted diseases) are now known among health workers as STIs (sexually transmitted infections) as they are *not* diseases and the term STIs is becoming more widely used than STDs.

2 Butterworth, J. *Thrush and its Treatment,* HarperCollins, Sydney, 1998, recommends that, in addition to treatment with antifungals, some women will receive relief from vaginal itching by douching with plain natural yoghurt.

INDEX